In Remembrance

Thomas E. Steere

# Charles Kuralt's
## American Moments

*Also by Charles Kuralt*
*in Large Print:*

Charles Kuralt's America
A Life on the Road
On the Road with Charles Kuralt

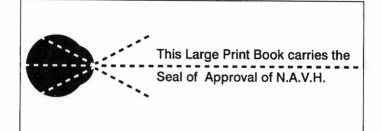

This Large Print Book carries the
Seal of Approval of N.A.V.H.

# Charles Kuralt's
## American Moments

*EDITED AND
WITH A PREFACE BY*

## PETER FREUNDLICH

*FOREWORD BY*

## CHARLES OSGOOD

**Thorndike Press • Thorndike, Maine**

Copyright © 1998 by Estate of Charles Kuralt

William Butler Yeats' "The Wild Swans at Coole" reprinted
with the permission of Scribner, a division of Simon & Schuster,
from *The Collected Works of W.B. Yeats, Vol. I: The Poems,*
revised and edited by Richard J. Finneran. Copyright © 1983,
1989 by Anne Yeats.

Special thanks to Ninth Wave Productions, Inc. for generously
providing the pictures for this book.

Published in 1999 by arrangement with Simon & Schuster, Inc.

Thorndike Large Print ® Basic Series.

The tree indicium is a trademark of Thorndike Press.

The text of this Large Print edition is unabridged.
Other aspects of the book may vary from the original edition.

Set in 16 pt. Plantin by Warren S. Doersam.

Printed in the United States on permanent paper.

**Library of Congress Cataloging in Publication Data**

Kuralt, Charles, 1934–
    Charles Kuralt's American moments / edited and with a
preface by Peter Freundlich ; foreword by Charles Osgood.
       p.  cm.
    Originally published: New York : Simon & Schuster, 1998.
    ISBN 0-7862-1790-1 (lg. print : hc : alk. paper)
    ISBN 0-7862-1791-X (lg. print : sc : alk. paper)
    1. United States — Description and travel — Anecdotes.
2. United States — Social life and customs — 1971– —
Anecdotes. 3. United States — Biography — Anecdotes.
I. Freundlich, Peter. II. Title. III. Title: American moments.
    [E169.04.K874   1999]
    973.92—dc21                                        98-32380

# Contents

## *American Emblems*

## American Originals

## American Portraits

## *American Shrines*

# American Makers

# American Dreamers

# American Sights

# American Heirlooms

## American Ways

# American Notions

# Preface

Admiration is something we are in desperately short supply of these days. We tend to diminish, rather than to enlarge, to minify, rather than magnify, whatever is good. Especially television news, in which Charles Kuralt worked all those years, and in which I still do work, makes the good small, and the bad as large as possible, on the theory that the surest way to attract the greatest attention is to frighten and alarm. A siren turns more heads than birdsong does, after all, and that is as it should be, provided that the danger of which the siren warns is real. The trouble is that, very often just now, the danger *isn't* real. This is the Age of the False Alarm, deliberately sounded by people who are in the crowd-gathering business.

On the other side, however, all alone for nearly four decades, representing something else entirely, was Charles Kuralt, who set off *away* from the sirens and the crowds and the pitchmen and the barkers for whom those crowds had been assembled, to find antidotes to the pervasive illness we didn't even know we had — antidotes in the form of quiet, truthful, beautifully told and shaped stories about the best in us, and about people so unself-regarding that they themselves did not know, until Charles held the mirror up to them, that there was anything *to* admire. This he did *thousands* of times, on *television*, for heaven's sake — which is like saying that, in the middle of Times Square on New Year's Eve, without raising his voice, he somehow managed to make himself heard on the other side of the country.

He *did* make himself heard — in the most deafening and the most deadeningly noisy medium human beings ever have devised, he made himself heard. His wonderful voice had something to do with that, of course. But what would his voice have been without the precision of his words, and his enormous intelligence, and his unerring ability to see directly into — and to express — the meaning of what he had discovered out there in the heart of the country? And then what would his voice have been without the quality I am still trying to explain — his capacity for admiration of, and his ability to make us admire, too, whittlers, fiddlers, stonecarvers, sharecroppers, bridge- and wall- and road-builders, kite flyers, sling shooters, coal miners, canal men, cowboys, raisers of crops and of children and of hope.

Charles and I came to work together in radio at first, and then in television on one broadcast or another. By the time he died, we had known each other for almost twenty years. These Moments were the last broadcasts he did, and the last on which he and I collaborated. They came into being after some gentlemen from Texas called Charles out of the blue to propose that he go on telling his stories of America — he had left CBS by then — in a series of ninety-second-long broadcasts to be distributed to independent television stations around the country. Charles declined. He didn't think ninety seconds was time enough in which to do anything worthwhile. But he gave the men from Texas my name anyway, probably because he didn't want to sound as if he were rejecting the idea flat-out; he had a hard time saying no to people.

When my call from Texas came, I declined too, for the same reason Charles had. But I began to ask myself where it was written that the smallest increment of television time — the lowly minute — automatically and forever had to be given over exclusively to nothing more than the pot-banging and horn-blowing of the commercial. Why couldn't we reclaim one turn and a half of the stopwatch for something better? Poems are often short, haiku always.

In the end, I convinced myself, and then Charles, that it wasn't impossible and that, moreover, it would be good at least to try. So we *did* try — one hundred and seventeen times, weighing our words with a diamond scale, to tell, in no time at all, stories of the American spirit and people and land that we hoped would dissolve in the bloodstreams of those who saw and heard them, there to have a somewhat longer-lasting effect than their mere ninety seconds would suggest.

Did we succeed? I don't know. As long as Charles was around, and I could see and hear him give these little essays life, I thought we had succeeded. Now I am not always sure. Sometimes I think what you have here are the clothes without the man in them, and not neatly displayed on hangers either, but just stepped out of and left on the floor. But then that may just be a measure of how much I miss him — or a measure of how flimsy my contribution seems to me without his to buttress it.

I find I haven't said anything about Charles the man. I suppose that is because he was as private a person as I ever met, and I know very well that he would not want me to be passing around verbal snapshots of him delighting my then five-year-old son by doing a little jig while balancing a pine cone on his head. (He actually did that, one day in Maine, which he had been in the habit of visiting long before we came to spend our vacations there.) But then he also would not have wanted me to produce these pages full of the praise to which, in many ways, he was allergic. Indeed, I have come to think that he was such an extraordinary admirer of others because, in the end, he thought so little of himself. He once said to me, lightly, with a smile and with charming self-deprecation, that he himself wasn't really good at anything. At first I thought he was just being modest. But I believe now he actually meant it, actually *didn't* value his prodigious gifts for writing and storytelling, and for making the stuff of real life into something very like poetry. This was why, I think now, he was so stunned by, say, the shipwright who could make a beautiful and shapely hull without using nails at all — as if Charles himself weren't doing the very same thing, fitting words and thoughts together without using nails at all, to make beautiful and shapely stories.

Enough. It's not as if I could bring him back by simply going on and on.

I'd say finally only this: I'm glad to have these Moments between hard covers. They need all the protection they can get.

PETER FREUNDLICH, JULY 1998

# Foreword

Cary Grant was once asked whether he realized that every man in the world wanted to be like him. The actor smiled that famous smile of his and said that, in a way, he could understand the feeling, since he too wished that he could be like Cary Grant. That is to say, he wished that he could be the Cary Grant the world knew — the dashingly handsome, unfailingly charming, daring, witty, and wonderful fellow we saw on the movie screen. But no flesh-and-blood human being could ever actually be such a paragon, of course. So here is the question. Can a flesh-and-blood human being actually have been Charles Kuralt?

Was he really the warm, wise, thoughtful, and sensitive wanderer we saw on the television screen? Was he in fact the sort of man he seemed to be, the sort of man who could talk with kings, presidents, or dirt-poor farmers and treat them all the same, a decent man who never lost the common touch and who loved his country not only for its great natural beauty, but also for the inner beauty and character of its people? Now comes the part where I pull away the veil to reveal the shocking, never-before-told truth: Yes, he was. Unlike Cary Grant, who seems not to have been Cary Grant, Charles Kuralt *was* Charles Kuralt.

He came across as a real, living, breathing, caring human being because he *was* a real, living, breathing, caring human being. But aren't all the people we see on television real, you ask? The answer, I fear, is no, they're not. A few are, but many are lacking the same vitally important body parts as the Scarecrow and the Tin Man were in *The Wizard of Oz*. You can trust me on this. I've been in the broadcast news business a long time. Charles's humanity was rare.

Despite that humanity, though, and his possession of a real brain and a real heart, there was one skill Kuralt possessed that seemed more than human to me. Charles Kuralt could write like an angel. Better than any of the rest of us. With a few well-chosen words spoken with more than a touch of North Carolina in that friendly, distinctive voice, Charles could make you laugh, make you cry; he could make you feel proud to be an American.

And while many of us in TV news were out there trying to expose somebody's mistakes or misdeeds or were trying to catch some high official with his pants down (that used to be just a figure of speech), Charles's joy was to show us something beautiful that someone did. Instead of trying to shock or dismay his viewers, Charles preferred to inspire us. The news might often be depressing, but Charles's stories would find something or somebody to restore our faith in human nature.

He was an explorer, Charles Kuralt was. And every explorer in a sense is trying to find himself. He lived in the city, but went out like a restless soul across the backroads of this country to see and hear and feel for himself what America was all about. He was proud to say that everywhere he went people told him he was welcome to come back. Not everybody in the news business can say that. People thought of him as a friend. Millions did, I suppose. But not very many people knew him very well.

Whether he finally found himself out there in America, I cannot say. But I know what he *did* find. He found *us*. No one in my time, no one on television, has shown ourselves *to* ourselves as truly, as lovingly, as skillfully, as memorably, as he did.

Was he also other than the man we watched on TV? Did he have flaws and imperfections, like the rest of us? Yes, of course.

But here is the amazing thing: Whatever *else* he may have been, Charles Kuralt really *was* Charles Kuralt.

Cary Grant would have been stunned.

CHARLES OSGOOD

# *American Emblems*

# The Cords of Winter

In New England, wood-stove country, a lot of people work for their winter warmth.

---

VERMONTER *I have some that I call "all- day suckers," because it will take some poor sucker all day to split it.*

There is a science to this: the right wood, split the right way, and stacked the right way, so that it will air-dry nicely. People's woodpiles say something about them. Most piles aren't "piles": they're beautiful, orderly sculptures.

But there are casual collectors of wood, too. If there's such a thing as a "chopaholic," for instance — someone who simply can't stop chopping — one of them may live here. He started out all right, and then just kept on, out of the woodshed and all across the yard.

If it's solitude you're seeking, you can find it with an ax and chopping block.

**VERMONTER**  *Nobody bothers you when you're splitting wood, because they're afraid you'll ask them to help.*

There is something to be said for a thermostat. Turn it up, and there, you're warm. But there's no pride in it, as there is in a fine winter woodpile. And I'm sure you know the old adage, common to many countries and many languages: "Who splits his own wood warms himself twice."

# Wind and Water

Around Lubbock, Texas, and in the other places of this country where there's still more horizon than anything else, this is the great *vertical* sight to see. To passers-through, the windmills of the West are beautiful symbols. To ranchers, like Carl Woods, they're much more than that.

---

WOODS *They're romantic, I suppose, and in the sunset, the windmill turning, etc., etc., etc. That's nice. But, to us, they're functional.*

This is their function: to bring water up from underground. The covered wagon may have *brought* us West, but the windmill made it possible for us to *stay*.

A windmill is a giant exclamation mark. It says, "Look here, in this remote place someone chose to make a life. I brought the water. Without me there would be no cattle, no ranchers, no families, no towns. Without me there would be no American West."

I think of those verses of Ecclesiastes the folk singer Pete Seeger set to music years

ago: "To everything — turn, turn, turn — there is a season; and a time for every purpose under heaven." Under the heaven of the Plains, in every season, there are windmills — turn, turn, turn.

# Fun on the Hoof

We're in Worcester, Massachusetts. And what miracle of the Machine Age is being made here, do you suppose? Wait, those look like horseshoes. And they *are*. But not bound for any hoof. These are pitching horseshoes, St. Pierre pitching horseshoes, if you please — the choice of champions for generations now, and the choice of presidents. That's Harry Truman in the middle there, watching a soldier who was so good that he could pitch ringers blindfold. Edward St. Pierre says all this goes back to ancient Rome.

---

ST. PIERRE *The Roman soldiers' horses had these disks on, like horseshoes. And they would fall off, and the peasants would pick them up. And that's what really started the game of horseshoes.*

Horseshoe pitching is a thoroughly American pastime now. And those who are serious about it covet *these*. Perfectly matched and balanced horseshoes have

helped make the old game more popular than ever.

I have met some country horseshoe pitchers who can pick up a couple of these, take you out behind the barn, and routinely throw ten ringers in a row. If you're pitching for money, make that twenty!

# Under the Big Top

The little town of Baraboo, Wisconsin, once was home to the gaudiest imaginations this country has ever known. Home, that is, to the Ringling Brothers.

---

FRED DAHLINGER  *Their father had come here to set up a harness-making shop, and it was here in 1884 in the spring when they staged the first performance of their circus.*

Fred Dahlinger, librarian at the Circus World Museum of Baraboo, can tell you all about how the Ringling boys got started. And he can tell you what their circus became.

---

DAHLINGER *Eventually it grew to be one hundred and seven double-length railroad cars. It's the greatest traveling entertainment amusement ever conceived by mankind.*

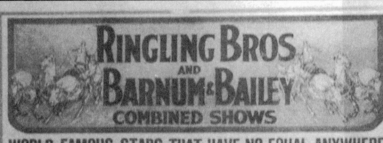

# RINGLING BROS
## AND
# BARNUM & BAILEY
### COMBINED SHOWS

## WORLD FAMOUS STARS THAT HAVE NO EQUAL ANYWHERE

**MAY WIRTH**

The Greatest Bareback Rider That Ever Lived

and the

**WIRTH FAMILY**

More Than **70** Mixed Equestrian Champions United in the Most Brilliant and All-Inclusive Displays Ever Assembled

"PHIL the Marvel"

**DAINTY MISS LEITZEL**

The World's Most Marvelous Lady Gymnast

CASTING HER BODY OVER HER

The Ringling Circus certainly was that. Into the small towns of America, where one day was very much like another, suddenly there came caravans, camels, elephants, a spangled army of occupation. If spaceships were to land on your front lawn right now — make that *hundreds* of spaceships — you might have some idea of the effect, at the turn of the last century, when the circus came to town.

There was nothing like it. To tell you the truth, there still isn't. Television is nice. But when was the last time television made your eyes shine, or made your jaw drop? The circus did that every day.

# The Little Red Wagon

Here is a question for you: can a sheet of metal make a child happy? Well, no.

But stamp that sheet of metal into a certain shape, refine it a little, then paint it and stencil the right name on its side — now your sheet of metal *can* make a child happy.

Which was just exactly what an immigrant carpenter named Antonio Pasin had in mind when he began making these little red wagons . . . eighty years ago.

---

ROBERT PASIN *One of my earliest memories is of being pulled along in a Radio Flyer wagon with my brothers and sister.*

Now Robert Pasin and his brothers run the company their grandfather founded. Antonio Pasin, once of Italy, then of Chicago, figured he could make wagons the way Henry Ford made cars — efficiently, on an assembly line. That way, they would be affordable. After all, what good was such a gleaming wonder if only little Lord Fauntleroys could afford them? Antonio

37

Pasin wanted the Huck Finns of this county to have little red wagons, too.

Just think what a child needs to transport every day: his bug collection, his basketball, his family dog, his kid brother, spare parts for wooden swords, and space helmets. Without a little red wagon, a kid would be lost.

# The Once and Future Fair

You know, of course, that the twenty-first century is just around the corner. But look here: the nineteenth century is quite nearby, too.

Go to a state fair and you'll see and hear just what your grandparents saw and heard when *their* parents took them to the fair. You'll see livestock being gussied and groomed — that hasn't changed. You'll see

pink pigs, blue ribbons, and brown cows. You will see pride. And cockiness. If ever an old-timer buttonholes you to tell a story of this country that begins "Time was . . . ," you can say, "Oh, it still is."

It still happens that crowds wait tensely for word from the judges. It still happens that the hometown favorite, furry or feathered, must face the favorites of other hometowns. And it still happens that night comes to the fair. This is not history. This is now.

You can visit the past by opening a book. Or you can close your eyes and listen for a brass band, a calliope, a rooster crowing, a child laughing. Hear any of that, and head for the source. You'll find yourself at the fair.

# The Last of the Red, White, and Blue

**BOB MARVY** *We've been making barber poles since 1950. The first barber pole was created in my parents' house, and my brother and I actually turned on the switch that started that pole.*

So this all began in 1950 — and nearly ended a decade or so later when those mop tops got off the plane.

**MARVY** *When the Beatles came to the United States, that changed the entire barber industry.*

If you doubt that the Beatles changed hairstyles in this country, notice the shoulder-length haircut of the Marvy Company employee at work here.

Some version of this symbol is as old as the Middle Ages, when barbers did tooth-pulling and surgery, too, and customers knew where to find them by the white towels stained red that they set to flapping in the wind outside their shops.

Nowadays, many men have their hair *styled*, not cut, at salons where cappuccino is served and music is played. So it has come down to this: the Marvy Company of St. Paul, Minnesota, is the last remaining maker of barber poles in all of America.

Bob Marvy means to go on. Of course he does. Who better than a maker of barber poles to understand the cycles of fashion and business. Bob Marvy can see the truth of that old expression right in front of him every day. What goes around, comes around.

# Sentinels of the Desert

Show this picture to anyone, anywhere, and the instant response will be, "Ah, the American West." This is America at a glance, as much as the Statue of Liberty is, or the Washington Monument.

In all the world, the giant saguaro cactus grows in profusion only here in the Sonoran Desert of Arizona and northern Mexico. In this lonely place, as park ranger Jeff Wallner can tell you, the saguaros are company, somehow.

---

WALLNER *People compare these to themselves. You know, they've got the upraised arms, they look a little humanlike.*

They grow the way we do, too. A forty-year-old cactus is about as tall as a forty-year-old man. But then *they* go on growing, taller and older. Some have grown to fifty feet and lived for two centuries.

Saguaros are a welcome sight to bats and bees and birds who feed on their flowers, and for human beings the great cactuses

lend towering majesty to a vast landscape.

"Sentinels of the Desert" is what some people call the saguaros. These sentinels have seen everything, from nomadic native tribes to conquistadors clanking north, to cowboys on the trail. A lot of history.

But the saguaros are silent. They keep it all to themselves.

# Proof Through the Night

There may not be a more American place anywhere than the one you're looking at. Not because Annin & Company in New Jersey has been the source of a river of red, white, and blue since its founding in 1849. Annin *is* the oldest and largest flag maker in America.

Its flags have flown at every inauguration since Zachary Taylor's, and at the North Pole, and the South Pole, and on the moon.

But look around. A woman of China sews flags here. And a man of Haiti rivets them. A

worker from Burma folds the flags, and another from Ecuador sees to the stars. They are from everywhere.

You know how fabric is made, of threads laced together so that the whole is stronger than any of its parts. Who are these workers but the threads of our fabric?

This is not the dawn's early light nor twilight's last gleaming, but there is something to hail here nonetheless among these flagmakers who are a living flag themselves.

Does the star-spangled banner yet wave o'er the land of the free and the home of the brave? Ask the workers at Annin & Company. They'll tell you.

# A Stone Wall

If you go for a walk in the woods in any northern place in America, sooner or later you'll come across what we came across in these woods — an old stone wall. Fifty or a hundred or two hundred years ago, somebody clearing a field picked up every one of these stones and carried them a distance and made a wall of them here. Whatever else he did here, the forest shrugged off long ago. But the wall remains.

Other countries have ruined castles, pyramids, and Parthenons. We have these grown-over monuments to forgotten farmers. The wall names no names, but whispers much about what must have been. There must have been a homestead and apple trees, a barn, children playing once their chores were done. All that must have been, or why this wall?

With enough research into local history, I might have been able to tell you who built that stone wall. But I like leaving the history there in the woods where the moss and the dragonflies know it, and the rain and the snow know it, even if we don't.

# Still Humming Along

Since 1916, these old machines, driven by leather belts, have been turning out unique bits of Americana. The corporation president, David Berghash, in the foreground here, does not mind blowing his own horn.

BERGHASH  *We are the only metal kazoo manufacturer in the world. We make the four-and-a-half-inch submarine-shaped kazoo, that's the little one. We also make the trombone kazoo, which is metal, the trumpet kazoo, and the bugle kazoo.*

An immigrant clockmaker named Von Klegg seems to have come up with the idea about 1850. By rights, therefore, this musical instrument that anyone can play ought to be called a Vonkleggophone. But "kazoo" it is. The name itself was trade-marked long ago right here at this factory in Eden, New York, out of which building-sized horn of plenty, horns aplenty have come for eighty years.

BERGHASH *Great going, guys.*

It is shiny, pocket-sized, and inexpensive, and entirely unpretentious: as democratic and all-American a little music maker as you can imagine. If you can carry a tune, you can play a kazoo. If you *can't* carry a tune, by the way, as I can't, a kazoo can't help you much.

# Fenders and Flaps

May I have a word with you about progress? Look at the cars we drive now, and look at *these* cars. Look at the airplanes in which we fly, and those in which we used to fly.

We are at the Owls Head Transportation Museum of Owls Head, Maine. Really, this place ought to be called the Museum of Derring-Do. Look how we used to get around, once upon a time.

But what we had more of once upon a time was — brass. Once upon a time, we had a lot of brass, which is just exactly what it takes to go rumbling along the roads in these machines. Or to go aloft in these.

Our planes and cars are faster and safer and stronger, yes. In those areas, we *have* made progress. But in the so-beautiful-it-bowls-you-over department, I think we haven't made any progress at all.

Do you suppose the brand names of our day will make hearts beat fast a hundred years from now? Maybe they will, but surely not as fast as Stutz Bearcat, and Stearman, and Pierce-Arrow. Never mind driving one; it's a pleasure just to say those words, Stanley Steamer.

# Candy Clouds

What are all these people staring at?

They are staring at Becky Davis, traveling confectioner of Tennessee. Becky Davis may have the sweetest view of life anyone can have. She is a cotton candy maker.

DAVIS *Not everyone gets to watch a baby taking its first bite and deciding whether he likes it or not. Some nights I make up to a thousand bags in one night. People like to watch me flip it, and they like to watch me get covered with cotton candy.*

And then they like to get all covered with cotton candy themselves. Hard as it may be to believe, we didn't always have cotton candy. The stuff was invented — by a dentist, one account says — in the 1920s. A big puff of sugar, lighter than air and stickier than a paste pot — it was a sensation. Watching everybody watching Becky Davis, I'd say it still is.

And I wonder . . .

I wonder what people ate at fairs and carnivals before cotton candy came along.

# For Whom the Bell Tolls

AL QUINTANA *It's not like a saxophone or any other musical instrument. It's a percussion instrument.*

Here comes one of the percussion instruments Al Quintana is talking about. Al Quintana drives a cable car in San Francisco. The cable cars would be nothing without the cable car bells.

QUINTANA *A drummer once told me that every paradiddle and flamadiddle, and whatever kind of diddles they have, is derived off of a drum roll, so if you can get a good drum roll going, you can do just basically anything.*

Al Quintana's concerts are very well attended, all day long, uphill and down. Cars go by, buildings go by, the time goes by . . . and the authentic music of San Francisco goes by, too — played by a master.

Al Quintana would have better hours if he did another kind of work.

QUINTANA *You can drive a bus and be off Saturdays and Sundays and holidays. It's not my cup of tea.*

Of course it isn't — buses don't have bells.

QUINTANA *This is the end of the line, and the end of your ride.*

Ask not for whom the bells tolls. If you have reached your stop, it tolls for thee.

# The Great American Hat

HATMAKER *They say a cowboy, the last thing he takes off at night is his hat, and the first thing he puts on in the morning is his hat.*

COWBOY *It hangs right there. I've got a little hook right there next to my bed.*

Wearing a hat like one of these is as good as showing your passport anywhere in the world. The movies are responsible for that, of course. Out there in the dark, for nearly a century now, people everywhere have been looking up at — looking up *to*, really — tall figures in tall hats. Now in Namibia, as much as here in New Mexico, these hats mean something.

HATMAKER *Oh, all self-respecting cowboy hats have bows on them. They have to, or you're not a cowboy.*

Did she say "self-respecting"? That is about as close as you can get to the meaning of this

symbol in a word.

I met a long-haired hippie one time who said he was hassled by the cops in every town he passed through on a cross-country motorcycle trip. Then he bought a cowboy hat. He wasn't a long-haired hippie after that. He was a long-haired cowboy. Nobody bothered him anymore.

# *American Originals*

# Landing for Lunch

The lunch-hour rush is over now at the Summit House of Beaumont, Kansas, so the crowd is taking off — literally, taking off.

Most days there are more airplanes in the parking lot here than cars. Pilots like the food at the Summit House, of course. But there is something else about the place they like.

---

PILOT *It's pretty neat taxiing an airplane down the road, coming up to a stop sign, pulling over to eat dinner. It's all right.*

Is that Main Street, or a taxiway? It's both, actually, which is why pilots have to be mindful of the rules of the road.

---

MAN *He got a ticket for not stopping at this stop sign.*

We drivers take for granted being able to pull right up to a diner. But that is a rare treat for a pilot, and reason enough, it seems, to file a flight plan and fire up the engine.

Steve Cutright works at the Summit House.

CUTRIGHT *It's surprising how many people will fly in just to have a cup of coffee and piece of pie, then fly out. I came in here one Saturday; there were two full-sized airplanes down, seven ultralights landing, two more planes, two mules, and a horse within about an hour and a half.*

Let your flaps down, Captain. I see hash browns at two o'clock.

In this part of Kansas, a hearty meal never is far away, as the crow flies.

Watch out for the stop sign on Main Street, though.

PAUL BUNYAN
MOTEL
ON LAKE BEMIDJI

BEST RATES
LAKEVIEW ROOMS
WKLY MONTH RATE

# Our Great Woodsman

Here's a Minnesota travel tip for you. To get to the Paul Bunyan Motel, or the Paul Bunyan Sub Shop, just drive along the Paul Bunyan Expressway until you get to Paul Bunyan Drive. You'll know it's Paul Bunyan Drive — Paul Bunyan is standing there as a crossing guard.

Proceed from that Paul Bunyan to the next Paul Bunyan, and the next. If you come to Paul Bunyan's sweetheart Lucette, or to Paul Bunyan, Junior, or to Paul Bunyan and Babe, his blue ox, you have gone too far. In that case look for the Paul Bunyan State Trail and follow *it* for a while.

In Bemidji, Minnesota, which calls itself the birthplace of Paul Bunyan, and in other towns nearby, you never can go too far without seeing some sign of the great woodsman of American folklore.

His stride, it is said, took in twenty-four townships at a time. And a dance he held once caused an earthquake that moved a river three counties to the east.

"Who made Paul Bunyan?" was the question the poet Carl Sandburg asked. "Who joked him into life amid axes and trees, saws and lumber?"

*We* made him, is the answer. Carved him out of our own pride. And then out of wood, too.

# Upright Announcements

See one of these, and you know at once where you are. But what do the wonderful, gaudy totem poles of Alaska mean? Lee Heinmiller can tell us. He has been working with totem pole carvers for decades.

HEINMILLER    *There are mortuary poles, which are to commemorate someone's death. A lot of the poles are storytelling poles, because Tlingit was an oral tradition, not a written language. And so it's a visual aid to remember a story. Sometimes there are clan poles, and then poles to commemorate specific events. If your daughter married the chief's son and you wanted to remember and commemorate the event, you could do a large totem.*

So totem poles are upright announcements — of births and marriages and deaths, of family pride and lineage. And sometimes, as carver Clifford Thomas admits, they're just for showing off!

THOMAS   *I'm a Tlingit under the Whale House, but if I was to show wealth, I'd hire the opposite tribe, Eagle, somebody in the Eagle side to carve me a pole.*

Down in the Lower Forty-eight, folks might buy a big car to impress the neighbors. The Tlingits do it better, don't you think?

# No Large Envelopes, Please

If form follows function, as the architects say, then a building in which stamps are canceled ought to be stamp-sized. And this one is, relatively speaking. The post office of Ochopee, Florida, is the smallest in all this country.

But Postmaster Naomi Lewis likes this cozy place of hers. Of course she does: It fits her like a glove. Well, like a glove *box*.

Whoa, easy: there's a post office behind you, you know.

They're not going to get all of *that* mail into this place, are they? I hope no good citizen of Ochopee has mail-ordered a refrigerator — or an extra-large book.

You'll notice that around here they use the *five-* and not the nine-digit zip code. Where would they put the other four digits? And notice, too, that customers don't exactly go *into* the Ochopee post office. They sort of stand up against it, on the doorstep, where there's room.

And there *are* customers, quite a few when the tourists stop to buy souvenir postcards. Those postcards have almost life-sized pictures of the post office on them.

# The Heights of Technology

This is not the first Ferris wheel. The *first* Ferris wheel, constructed by the engineer George Washington Gale Ferris, was the talk of the Chicago World's Fair of 1893.

But look at it another way. *Every* Ferris wheel is *someone's* first. So if you want to see what sort of effect the very first wheel had a century ago, just watch the faces of these riders at the South Florida State Fair.

Remember this: There were no tall buildings in the small towns of this county in 1893, and only a very few even in its large cities. Nor were there any flying machines. Americans never really had looked down on their country before Mr. Ferris's wheel came along.

It's hard to put into words. John Shuler's words are as good as any.

---

SHULER *It goes way up. You can see the whole park.*

That's the thing about a Ferris wheel. It goes way up.

A hundred years ago the wonderful machinery and struts and trusses of the Ferris wheel represented state-of-the-art science in the service of pure joy. Progress and pleasure were hand in hand at last.

# At the Market

The story of Seattle's Pike Place Market is a story of loaves and fishes. Of cabbages and kings — well, king crabs. Of fruit and flowers, of acres of oysters and mountains of ice. Of Polish pastries and northwestern chowder. It is the story, in other words, of this country's rich harvests.

Rich harvests of people, too. Josie Pinor has been here since 1952.

PINOR  *I grew up in the market.*

Mike Manza grew up at the market, too.

MANZA  *My grandfather used to come from South Park in a horse and buggy when it was all farmers.*

Walk around Pike Place early in the morning and you will find the bounty of the sea, and the bounty of the fields.

The streets of America are not paved with gold. But the old stories of the wealth of this land were not so wild after all.

On this earth are millions of people, tens of millions of people, who never have seen nor ever will see the kind of abundance that is everyday and ordinary at the Pike Place Market.

And the Pike Place Market is only a corner of a corner of a corner of America.

# Lucy

Here are the classic makings of a day at the shore: surf, sand, beach houses, a wooden elephant . . .

Wait, perhaps we've had too much sun. Better look again. Surf, sand, beach houses, and, yes, that definitely is a building shaped like an elephant. Lucy by name: a pachyderm of wood and steel, built here in Margate City, New Jersey, in 1881 for a local land speculator.

Lucy was a hotel at the turn of the century. Then she was a tavern, which would have reversed the usual order of things. You aren't supposed to begin seeing elephants until you *leave* the pub.

As for that old observation about the eyes being the windows of the soul, Lucy's eyes really *are* windows.

I love Lucy, and have visited her several times. Some attractions haven't a leg to stand on. Lucy has *four* — one with a *door* in it.

Lucy's howdah — the howdah is that platform up there on the roof — was refurbished

recently at a cost of more than thirty thousand dollars. The sum should not be a surprise. After all, what do we call a rare and unusual possession that is expensive to maintain? You know. A white elephant.

# A New Dish

Now, about Buffalo wings: did you think they were whimsically named for bison? Come then to the city of Buffalo, and to the Anchor Bar of Buffalo, where you can hear about the very night it happened.

Pat Marchiello is a regular at the Anchor, to say the least.

MARCHIELLO *I've been coming to the Anchor Bar probably fifty-seven years.*

One night in 1964, late, Pat and the son of owners Frank and Teresa Bellissimo, and some other friends, came in hungry. Teresa said she'd see what there was. But all she had were some chicken wings set aside for making soup. Inspiration seized Teresa Bellissimo. She barbecued the wings, and whipped up a sauce, and a new dish was placed on the American table.

MARCHIELLO *That was the first night we had the chicken wings here.*

*Bellissimo,* Frank and Teresa. Well done. And one order medium well done, too, please.

You can get Buffalo wings now in Bangor and Baton Rouge and Boise and Bakersfield. It used to be that people threw the wings out. Now they can't serve them fast enough.

And notice one other thing. In Buffalo, they're called "chicken wings." In France, you know, they don't call those potatoes "French fries" either.

# The Lincoln Highway

Do you know what that *L* there stands for? It stands for everything we have come to stand for. In this nation of highways, the Lincoln Highway came first.

It was a wildly audacious idea of 1913, to widen and straighten and pave, and then to link the Main Streets of America, and the little trails that went nowhere, to make a path for the motorcar from New York to California.

How'd they do it, Frank Roza, in your part of Nebraska?

ROZA  *By hand.*

Brick by brick, by shovel and wheelbarrow, they went clear across the county.

But not much of the Lincoln Highway remains. It's buried now beneath newer stretches of road, or bypassed. The way west has fallen by the wayside.

This seventy-year-old guidebook to the Lincoln Highway recommends taking supplies along on your drive from coast to coast: loaves of bread, dozens of eggs. But diners would spring up soon enough. And billboards and gas stations. Modern America itself would spring up soon enough.

We are a roadside nation now. The Lincoln Highway was the road that made us one.

# A Burst of Speed

Jack Keetley lasted the whole grueling eighteen months. Johnny Fry was first. The Fisher boys were part of it, too.

Part of what? The wildest relay race ever conceived. The Pony Express. Mail delivered overland from Missouri to California, two thousand miles, in ten days, for five dollars a half ounce.

It began right in this building in St. Joseph, Missouri. Gary Chilcote is the director of the Patee House Museum, which houses the Pony Express Museum.

---

CHILCOTE *They rode through Kansas and Nebraska, dipped into Colorado and across Wyoming, and Nevada and Utah, and dropped down into California.*

*The old sign on the wall reads: "Wanted — Young, Skinny Wiry Fellows, Not over Eighteen, Must Be Expert Rider. Willing to Risk Death Daily. Orphans Preferred. Wages, $25 a Week. Apply at the Pony Express Office."*

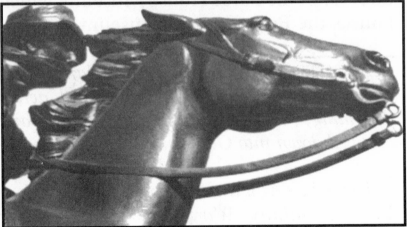

The enterprise lasted only a year and half, but it was an amazement. Night and day, from ramshackle station to ramshackle station, teenaged daredevils kept distant California in touch with the Union. And that kept California *part* of the Union.

Then, with the completion of the transcontinental telegraph, it all ended. The country got in a great adventure — just under the wire.

# The Barbershop Blues

What we see all the time we stop seeing, if you know what I mean. Take this blue liquid. Did you even know what it was called? Barbicide. Made for fifty years at King Research of Brooklyn, New York, first by its inventor, Maurice King, and now by his son, Ben.

At the barbershop we do not focus on it; we simply know it's there and are reassured. But visitors to the Smithsonian Institution in Washington will be focusing on Barbicide — a jar of the stuff has gone on display there. And why is that, Ben King?

KING  *It has replaced the barber pole as a symbol.*

A symbol of America's resolve to banish the germ from the comb and the brush.

By the way, if his barber had not scratched and nicked him quite so often, Maurice King might have come up with another name. "Barbicide," you see, means . . .

KING *Kill the barber.*

He wasn't serious about that, of course.

Fifty years later you see it everywhere. His family's product has become an institution. Now Ben King would like that institution joined to another institution of America. He dreams of a crayon of a new color: "Barbicide Blue."

# *American Portraits*

# A Man of the Road

Highwaymen of old were figures to fear, but here's a highwayman to admire. For thirty years, on his own time, at his own expense, Tom Weller's been driving the roads of Southern California in search of people to help. He does this because, long ago, someone once helped him.

WELLER  *I asked what I owed him. He said you just help somebody else you come across in trouble.*

He's helped thousands of people by now — people out of gas or oil or water, people with flat tires. You know, to sit in a stalled car on the highway can be life-threatening. Tom Weller gets people out of harm's way. Doing that, he has saved lives.

His car's a '55 Ford — mostly.

WELLER  *This is a '56 Mercury station wagon bumper. This is a '60 Dodge Phoenix taillight. The roof rack is a '68 Chrysler.*

But the heart of all this is Tom Weller's heart.

WELLER *Every time I help someone else, it helps me. Lifts my spirits.*

He lifts our spirits, too. Tom Weller accepts no payment for what he does. Helping is his pleasure. Says so right here on the little cards he puts in people's hands, just before he smiles and drives off to go help someone else.

# Lions and Tigers and Bears

Do you know what Irving Chais does in the cluttered little shop he took over from his father fifty years ago? The sign on the door does not say enough. It ought to say "Mender of Broken Hearts."

---

CHAIS  *What happened to the ears?*

---

BOY  *I ate them.*

---

CHAIS  *You ate them?! [Laughs.]*

Here is a man who can take a child's most cherished companion, or an adult's, and make it new again.

Irving Chais is a master restorer of dolls and stuffed animals, and a restorer most of all of the faith of their owners. After all, without his magic, they would be forced to feel that they had loved too well.

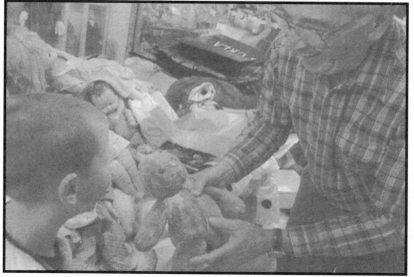

CHAIS *We have people that come in that are seventy-five, eighty years old that had a little teddy bear or a little dog, and they've had this little possession for all their lives.*

WOMAN *He's beautiful.*

CHAIS *People are basically children. Age does not make an adult.*

You're right, Mr. Chais. What makes us old is broken-heartedness. And that is something *you* can cure.

CHAIS *I loved working with him [he says of a stuffed pig]. He's very nice, he's very genteel.*

People walking *up* the single flight of stairs to Irving Chais's shop on the East Side of Manhattan tend to look forlorn and dejected. People walking *down*, however, don't. They have been given back a bit of the world as it used to be, when it and they were wide-eyed together.

# Mending Their Majesties

KIM MIDDLETON *This is our patient ward, where critical patients are kept.*

Patients? What patients could be kept there?

We are at the Alaska Raptor Rehabilitation Center — an emergency room for injured birds of prey. There are hawks here, and falcons, and owls; but most of the injured are eagles.

And how do eagles come to be injured? Sad to say, they hit things.

MIDDLETON *Vehicles, power lines, buildings, airplanes.*

Sometimes, even sadder to say, they *are* hit.

MIDDLETON *We do see a number of gunshot wounds and trapping injuries every year.*

Kim Middleton is curator here, and head nurse. If she were a royal physician, she could not have more majesty in her care. But from this majesty Kim Middleton averts her eyes. These emperors of the air would take it as a threat if she looked directly at them. Kings and queens are like that — even when they're ailing.

It isn't true that a bird in the hand is worth two in the bush. The bush is where they belong — the bush and the wide blue sky. The folks at the nursery at Alaska do everything they can to get their birds of prey out of hand as quickly as possible.

# The Sounds of Silence

This is a story about a collector of peace and quiet. Peter Acker calls himself a "natural sound preservationist." He records sounds without any of the ruckus and rhubarb of civilization. Sad to say, he has to go further and further afield — further astream in this case — to find the pure sounds of nature.

---

ACKER *In a lot of ways I feel like I'm in a race against humanity, you know, the expansion of humanity, to document these areas of natural quiet before they're gone.*

In this work, two heads really are better than one.

---

ACKER *This is Fritz. He hears as we hear.*

Only he — Fritz — has a microphone in each ear, so that others will be able to hear what he has heard.

Well. This is a story about quiet, so that's what I ought to be for a few seconds . . . quiet.

Peter Acker sells his recordings of peace and quiet. The sounds of jet planes and eighteen-wheelers are almost inescapable in this world, but thanks to this one man, not quite . . . not yet.

# A Man of Parts

RUSS VARNER *I have people peering in my windows most every day.*

Well, he has people peering *out* his windows most every day, too. Russ Varner's shop is crowded whether there are customers in it or not. He is a sculptor who restores mannequins for museums and department stores and the like.

VARNER *Every once in a while I have a person ask me what I do, and I tell them I'm a plastic surgeon. I work in plastics primarily, and I do a lot of alterations on body forms.*

He does what he does by himself, mostly, though every once in a while he does need a hand — or an arm. He is a disarming sort of fellow. Footloose, too, and a man of vision.

But in the end, when he is done, dummies that have been downsized after years of faithful service can look forward to many more years of standing firm wherever they are set down.

VARNER  They come in here and they get a new life to go out somewhere else.

To go out somewhere else, or to hang around.

Russ Varner probably meant to go into a more conventional sort of sculpting originally, but then he wouldn't have had the same body of work to show. And his prices would have been higher, too. His mannequins *don't* cost — an arm and a leg.

# Home, Tiny Home

You know how it is being a homeowner. There's always work around the house: a lamp to replace, or shingles to make, or windows to fix.

Ned Kellogg of Cold Spring Harbor, New York, has a Ph.D. in anatomy. Long ago, however, he turned into a home builder. Why build tiny houses instead of big ones, Mr. Kellogg?

---

KELLOGG *I first of all don't like going up ladders.*

Well, that doesn't explain the saintly patience this requires, or the surgeonly skill.

Ned Kellogg was a good carpenter even as a child. When he was small he built *big* things — full-sized furniture. Now that *he* is big, he builds *small* things — stunning small things.

You will notice that I have not called them dollhouses. They are far finer than that. Look at this half-timbered cottage of Shakespeare's day. Perfection is perfection, no matter the scale.

Ned Kellogg knows more about home-ownership than anyone else I can think of. After all, he owns dozens of homes. Until, that is, some buyer appears in his shop and falls in love, and decides to take one of Ned Kellogg's homes home.

# The Swift Completion

Huey Collins of Baldwin County, Alabama, is the mailman of the Magnolia River.

---

COLLINS  *Good morning, Mr. and Mrs. Wright!*

Mail has been delivered by boat hereabouts for most of this century. But not often, I'll bet, as neatly as *he* does it. Watch. He doesn't stop or bump the dock *ever*. He only glides deftly by, slowing his boat and quickening his hands.

Here is a difficult double stuff: the always tricky pickup *and* delivery. No problem. Nothing to it.

It is a water ballet Huey Collins does. Land-bound letter carriers have only dogs to worry about. Here, alligators are in a day's work.

---

COLLINS  *Up close, he's all right. He'll go about his business. As long as you don't jam them in a corner someplace, you know.*

*The mailman cometh!!*

119

And goeth. Talk about the swift completion of his appointed rounds.

Huey Collins took over that route of his just four years ago. Four short years, and there he is already, leaving other letter carriers in his wake.

# Big Ship, Small Shed

If you think building a ship in a bottle is a neat trick, come along to the Hodgdon Brothers boatyard of East Boothbay, Maine.

That's Tim Hodgdon, whose family has been building boats in these parts since 1816.

But this hull, begun upside down in the time-honored manner, is nearly as big as the shed that houses it. And now in this very tight space, it will have to be turned right side up.

We're making hours fly by in seconds here to show you a very rare American Moment. Even among veteran shipbuilders, few have seen such a thing done on such a scale.

Tim Hodgdon *did* allow himself a brief moment of pride when the great turning-over was done.

---

HODGDON  *It went off without a hitch, and we're very, very happy about the vessel being right side up.*

But he says he never was worried. It isn't that he has ice water in his veins. What he has in his veins is a century and a half of skill, and that will steady a man, the way a keel steadies a boat.

# Cold, and Colder Still

---

MIKE HILLMAN  *That sky is telling me one thing, that come tomorrow it's gonna be colder yet.*

Cold, and colder yet — that's the way Minnesotans like it. Here's what Mike Hillman did last winter.

---

HILLMAN  *February first it was fifty-nine below zero, and the weatherman said it was gonna get colder. That's when I decided to go down to Tower, because I was convinced that it was going to set a record. A lot of guys have to sit on flagpoles and do all kinds of crazy things to get in the* Guinness Book, *and for me all I had to do was take the tent and the camping stuff and head down to Tower and sleep out in a sleeping bag.*

All he had to do, he means, was camp out on the night the thermometer sank to a new all-time Minnesota record: sixty below. Mike Hillman happened to have a banana with him that night. In the morning he used

124

that banana to drive a nail through a plank of wood.

Minnesotans share their beautiful lakes with tourists in the summer, but they like it best when the lakes freeze and the tourists go home.

---

HILLMAN *The wintertime it gets back to being a wild place again. The tent is pitched, the bag is ready to go, I've got a nice fire going, waiting for the evening to come.*

Mike Hillman, a true Minnesotan. A chip off the old iceberg.

If you think you're cold this winter, think of the thermometer where Mike Hillman is. Your neck of the woods is probably balmy by comparison, though I know that's what they call cold comfort.

# *American Shrines*

# Sullivan's Island

The waves that wash this place wash Plymouth Rock, too, away to the north on the Atlantic coast. Nor is the sand different here. But if this was where you stepped foot in the New World, then you were coming not to freedom, but to bondage. This may be the saddest stretch of shore anywhere in all this land. This is Sullivan's Island, in the harbor of Charleston, South Carolina. From the 1670s to the 1770s, more slave ships came here than to any other port of America.

There were pest houses here, as they were called — buildings in which to quarantine the tens of thousands who came from Sierra Leone and Angola, and all the other areas of West Africa, until it could be determined that they were free of disease. Then they went on to the market on the mainland, where husbands might be sold to one bidder and wives to another and their children to a third. Here, on Sullivan's Island, many families were together for the last time in all their lives.

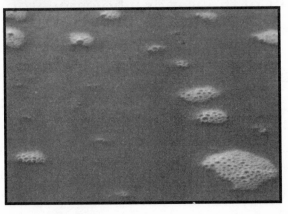

This moon looked down on a great shame of this country, and on terrible despair.

These are not salt tears on the soft sand of Sullivan's Island. But they ought to be.

# Noah Webster's House

MISS WAKEFIELD *Master Chris, the word is "public." [Children spell "public."]*

Here you have a class of children being taught to spell by a teacher named Miss Wakefield. *She* was taught to spell, we *all* were, by Noah Webster. It's *his* house the children are visiting in West Hartford, Connecticut, and *his* book they're using.

Noah Webster's blue-backed speller went everywhere with us when this country was growing up. In this speller of his, and later in the first American dictionary, Noah Webster did with words what the Minutemen did with muskets: declared us independent. He made us proud of purely American words like "hickory" and "skunk," and he taught us the American way to spell them and say them.

WAKEFIELD *Could you please spell "liberty." [Child misspells "liberty."] Okay, please sit down.*

It happens that George Washington himself was a good speller, and wanted his grandchildren to be good spellers, too. So he asked his friend, Noah Webster, to be their tutor, to teach them . . . right from "rawng."

# Mr. DeLeo's Monument

We all love the Statue of Liberty, of course, but not a one of us loves her as much as this man does. Charlie DeLeo first saw Lady Liberty as a schoolboy on a class trip. He left her that day, of course, as all visitors must. He grew up and went to Vietnam to serve his country.

Then he came back, to serve the *symbol* of his country. For twenty-five years, Charlie DeLeo has been Liberty Island's official, full-time Keeper of the Flame.

---

DELEO *I'm the only man to ever work on top of the golden flame and stand on top of it eight times.*

He keeps more than just the flame, you understand. Charlie DeLeo attends to the Statue of Liberty in all her glory. He adds to her luster, and she adds to his.

DELEO *To be Keeper of the Flame of the greatest monument in the world, that symbolizes freedom and democracy, is just really a blessing from God. I'm very, very proud.*

He takes care of her, she takes care of us. We all can rest easy.

What are those lines of Irving Berlin's: "Stand beside her, and guide her, through the night with the light from above." In our day the only man ever to have held a light to *her* light from above has been Charlie DeLeo, Keeper of the Flame.

# The Czar's America

Wait. This man looks like a Russian Orthodox priest. And surely these are icons of the Russian Orthodox Church. But we are collecting *American* Moments. Why are we in some province of Russia? Well, we're not. We are in Alaska.

This is St. Michael's Orthodox Cathedral, in Sitka. Sitka was the capital of Russian America. From the 1740s to the 1860s, the grandest of all the United States of America belonged to the czar. Alaska was *his* colony, full of his fur trappers and adventurers and missionaries. Islands hereabouts are named for them even now: Baranof, Kruzov, Kupranov. And Sitka still has a little of St. Petersburg about it. The old cathedral was consumed by fire thirty years ago. But the people of Sitka saved every relic there of Russian Alaska.

Lincoln's secretary of state, William Seward, championed the purchase of Alaska from the czar for the preposterously huge sum of $7,200,000. People called

Alaska "Seward's Folly" for a long time after that.

But go there sometime. Look around. The cost was about a cent and a half per acre. No greater beauty ever was bought for any price.

# When Shots Rang Out

Uh-oh, the time has come.

It comes on schedule every other Sunday, when the well-schooled volunteers of Tombstone, Arizona, reenact with relish a certain famous episode of their town's history, involving Doc Holliday and the Earp brothers on the side of the law, and the Clantons and McLaurys and Billy Clayburn on the other side.

By the way, the gunfight at the OK Corral took but half a minute. We can show you the whole thing.

Uh-oh, the time has come — again.

It was only thirty seconds of a day in 1881. But it was an American Moment to remember.

And Tombstone, Arizona, is not about to forget.

# Grant's Tomb

Imagine the Pyramids forgotten by the world, to become instead a local landmark of one little corner of the desert.

This place was a wonder of the world once, too. At the turn of the century, Grant's Tomb was New York's great tourist destination. And then, little by little, we forgot: forgot the War Between the States, forgot the general who ended that war, forgot the imposing memorial a grateful nation built to him. For years on end we forgot. General Grant belonged no more to the nation, but to the neighborhood.

That is changing. The tomb of General, and *President,* Ulysses S. Grant and of his wife, Julia, is in the care of the National Park Service now. From where *he* stands, ranger John Daskalakis can see the monument being scrubbed and repaired. And he believes he can see its future, too.

---

DASKALAKIS *I can imagine Grant's Tomb as inspiring as it was a hundred years ago. It was an amazing tribute to a great man.*

Workers are busy every day now, preparing for the hundredth anniversary this year of the dedication of Grant's Tomb. At the ceremony there will be crowds again in a place known for too long only to neighborhood mothers pushing their baby carriages, and to neighborhood children unaware of what a great spirit of America they were playing hide-and-seek with.

# At the Pump

Of the three simple words on this sign, one you just *think* you understand. "Ray" is Ray Bauernsmith, proprietor of this Chicago establishment. And "Auto," well, you know what an auto is. But "Service" may be something you've never actually had.

---

BAUERNSMITH  *We used to check the oil, wash the windows, check the battery, check the radiator . . .*

Things are different now, which is why Ray Bauernsmith has turned his shop into something like a museum of the Golden Age of the gas station. Language preserves things that have otherwise disappeared. We still talk about *pumping* gas. This is why: once upon a time, we *did*.

---

BAUERNSMITH  *You pumped.*

You could get a dollar's worth of Shamrock, or Liberty, or Bengal, and head off at a breakneck thirty miles an hour toward the next gas station, which might be shaped like a wigwam or a log cabin.

---

BAUERNSMITH *But that's all gone now.*

Language preserves things. We still call the places we pull into *service stations,* but just try to get a free calendar in one of *them.*

Ray Bauernsmith recalls that his regular customers used to hang around on Saturday and Sunday mornings after they'd had their fill-up. We seem to have lost sight of that part of what a car is good for — the stopping and getting out, and spending time, part.

# The Store That Was

Let's go shopping, shall we? Shopping for — another time.

Alexander Harkin opened his general store in Newton, Minnesota, in 1870. Newton was a riverboat town. Then the railroad came through, and the riverboats vanished, and Newton vanished with them.

But the Harkin family lived on in the house attached to the store. They stopped doing business — there was no business to do. Outside time passed. Inside — well, look around: about half the things on the shelves are pretty much where Alexander Harkin put them.

The Minnesota Historical Society owns the Harkin store now. We asked Opal DeWanz what a trip to Harkin's store might have set you back in 1870.

DEWANZ *A nickel at that time, well, it would have bought an inch of chewing tobacco, two pounds of flour.*

A visit to this store now will set you back a hundred years. Lest those prices make you too nostalgic, you should remember that nickels were hard to come by in those days.

And did you notice all the tonics and bitters and other nostrums? They were what we had instead of good doctors and good science. Ailments that we shrug off carried people away in 1870. A bottle of Dr. Jane's Tonic Vermifuge could only do so much.

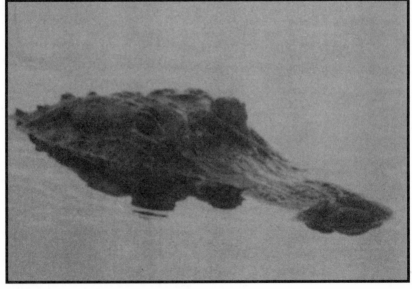

# The Ups and Downs
# of the Everglades

This is a story set in the Everglades of Florida, but it's not *about* the Everglades. Not really. It's about the delicate balance of things on our little planet.

Making their ways here are creatures of the water, and of the air, and of the air *boat*. That is Everglades Park ranger Su Jewell, who watches over this untouched place.

Did I say untouched? Well, what *is that?*

---

JEWELL  *It's about the only form of litter we find out here in the Everglades. It's a balloon, like those "I Love You" balloons that you find in a supermarket, or "Happy Birthday." People let them go, or they just escape on their own, so to speak, and they drift in the wind, and they end up in the Everglades. And out here where we have no public use, the only people that ever come out here are us. We find these balloons pretty much every time we come out. One less balloon polluting the Everglades.*

It seems you can stand in one place on this earth and pollute another place, by letting litter fall *up*.

It's true, the world *is* a delicate balance.

# Hanauma Bay

Would you care to see some denizens of the deep? At Hanauma Bay, on the island of Oahu, you only have to do what park volunteer Bob Gee is doing: just put your toes in the water. The denizens of the deep will meet you more than halfway.

---

GEE  *Now here's two of my very special friends, Toby and Ken, and they are Sailfish Tang.*

The fish are extraordinarily friendly here. They seem to know that no harm can come to them. Hanauma Bay is a preserve protected by the State of Hawaii, and by nature: these people are standing in the flooded bowl of an old volcano, barricaded across one end by a coral reef. Because the water is safe and calm, the fish can be frisky and curious.

In other places of this earth, you need a boat and gear and more than a little nerve to visit the floor of the sea. In this place, the floor of the sea visits you.

Where else was it that creatures so unlike one another got along so well? Oh yes, I remember now. I believe I'm thinking of the Garden of Eden. There are restrictions on what you're supposed to feed the fish at Hanauma Bay. But then, I seem to recall some sort of food restriction in the Garden of Eden, too.

# Land's End

Here at Cape Disappointment on the coast of Washington State, the greatest of all American journeys ended in 1805. The entry in the journals of Lewis and Clark says, "Ocean in view. Oh, the joy."

But other journeys had ended here already, and many more would end in the years to come. Sailors call this place "the graveyard of the Pacific." Two thousand ships have been wrecked in these waters; nearly as many lives have been lost.

The steep and headlong drop of the Columbia River into the sea makes the waves wild where river and ocean meet, and the wind makes the waves wilder. And the wild wind and the wild waves churn and shift the bar of sand in the channel that separates the river from the sea.

The name is not right, really. If the peril of the sea is what a sailor is looking for, Cape Disappointment never disappoints.

Ships still disappear off that cape. Last year at Thanksgiving a crab boat went down without loss of life — where a certain explorer might have seen it through his spyglass, while writing, "Ocean in view. Oh, the joy."

# A Railroad Palace

We love our cars, yes. But no one ever built a *garage* like this. This is the architect Jarvis Hunt's 1914 Union Station of Kansas City, Missouri. This magnificent railroad cathedral, closed for a decade, is being restored now, with the help, among others, of Andy Scott. He remembers what happened here the day word came of the attack on Pearl Harbor.

---

SCOTT *Pearl Bailey happened to be right here in the Grand Hall, and she literally stopped in her tracks and began singing "God Bless America," and hundreds of people around her did the same.*

Half the soldiers of this country passed through Union Station, Kansas City, by the time it was over over there. This was the way to war in those days.

The way west, too. And east, and north, and south. You know the expression "You can't get there from here." Well, from *here* you *could* get there.

SCOTT  *The idea was to create great grand buildings for everyday citizens.*

We love our cars. But look what we built for our trains.

Let your flight be delayed for an hour or two and all you have is time to waste.

Time between trains was time to *spend*.

# Rain Above, River Below

A covered bridge. But the scenery doesn't seem quite right for Vermont, nor for Pennsylvania. Where are we? Tell us, Bill Cockrell, of the *Oregon* Covered Bridge Society, why are bridges covered?

COCKRELL *When we built these bridges, it was to hold heavy weight, large trucks, wagons of hay or grain, and without a truss they would collapse. The real reason that we covered bridges is to protect those big timbers in the truss.*

Oregon, land of the big timbers, has more covered bridges than any other state west of the Mississippi. They were being built here when wood was all that was available. But then, well into the age of steel, too — though the last ones cannot have been built quite the way the first ones were.

COCKRELL *The old-timers who built bridges actually camped out at the bridge site. They fished and hunted, and they would contract with the farmers to provide eggs and meat and bread.*

So it was just a practical matter, really — a design meant to keep the weight-bearing timbers dry so they'd last longer. Nothing romantic about it at all.

But was there ever a prettier place to come in out of the rain than under a roof above a river?

*American Makers*

# The President's Shoes

It's one thing to say that Lyndon Baines Johnson's were big shoes to fill. It's another thing altogether to have made those shoes yourself.

Dominich DiMeola brought this skill with him from Italy. He brought his father's and grandfather's tools with him from Italy, too, to the venerable American shoemaking firm of Johnston and Murphy in Nashville, Tennessee. Johnston and Murphy made shoes by hand for Abe Lincoln. Dominich DiMeola, and then his protégé Raymond Robinson, continued that tradition of making shoes for the presidents of the United States.

------

DIMEOLA *We use some hard wax to wax the string, which makes it really, really sticky. See how sticky it is.*

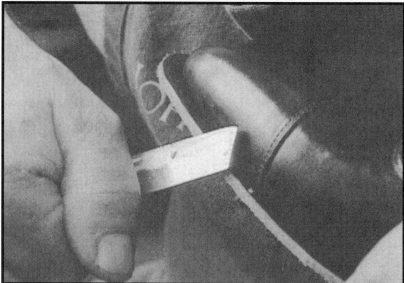

How they do what they do is with exquisite care. It takes eighty hours to make a shoe by hand. Harry Truman had a hard road to walk. Dominich DiMeola made the walking a little easier.

The rest of us would be ill shod without the good affordable shoes machines can make. But it's nice to know there's a man there in Nashville nailing one nail at a time, stitching one stitch at a time. They are shoes fit for a president. A president can't wear sneakers to the office, can he?

# Swept into Office

Make way for His Honor Bob Funke, mayor of the little town of Bishop Hill, Illinois — mayor . . . and broom maker.

---

FUNKE *I make a warehouse broom, a house broom, mother's helper's broom, fireplace broom, witch's broom, turkey-wing broom, and a colonial broom and a whisk broom.*

Once upon a time this part of Illinois was to brooms what Detroit is to cars. But broomcorn must be harvested by hand, and so the crop moved south to Mexico where they do all that cutting one stem at a time.

But Bob Funke still plants and cuts three acres of his own every season, mainly to keep the tradition alive.

If it's true that a new broom sweeps clean, then Bob Funke's little shed may be responsible for more cleanliness than any other space of its size anywhere.

Oh, one more thing. How do you judge a broom, Mr. Mayor?

FUNKE *A good broom stands alone.*

It's an old tradition the mayor of Bishop Hill is keeping up, old in this country, and ancient in the world. How do you imagine Joseph and Mary swept the manger? No doubt, with a bundle of broomcorn much like this one. It seems the simplest things survive the longest.

# Philip Simmons of Charleston

You've heard of the "Anvil Chorus." This is an anvil *soloist,* student of one of the greatest blacksmiths of our time, Philip Simmons. For seventy years at his anvil and forge, Philip Simmons has been turning iron into something like lace. There's an iron gate everywhere you look in old Charleston. It is commonly said that if it's a truly beautiful gate, it was made by an artisan of the eighteenth century, or it was made by Philip Simmons.

---

SIMMONS  *I came to Charleston at the age of eight for an education.*

He came here to *get* an education, but ended up *giving* one instead — a lifelong education in how to make beautiful shadows permanent.

SIMMONS *People will come by the shop and say, "Hey, Philip, say, you know the blacksmith's becoming a lost art?" I say, "Lost art? Always going to be something for the blacksmith to do."*

Scholars will tell you that the Iron Age began about two thousand years ago. As for when the Iron Age reached its peak, I'd say it hasn't yet. Philip Simmons is still at work. Though, really, he could rest now. His legacy is ironclad.

# A Maker of Whirligigs

You know how thrifty New Englanders are. They're not willing to waste anything — not even the wind. Joe Mulkhey of Maine is a master maker of whirligigs. I had a New England uncle like him whose whirligig carvings enchanted me when I was a little boy.

***

MULKHEY  *I've had kids giggle and laugh, and had adults do the same thing. It's kind of nice.*

Whirl, you whirligig horses. Play, you musicians. Full speed ahead, sternwheeler.

***

MULKHEY  *There was a time when these were made by people who had ordinary intelligence . . .*

That was in another age, when ordinary people had time. Now it takes someone out of the ordinary to make us see the wind, and hear it.

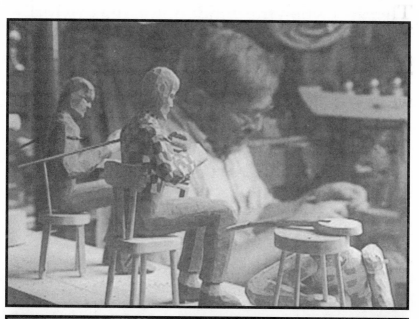

**MULKHEY** *Usually, after I finish one, I can't believe it'll really work.*

They say, "Make hay while the sun shines." Yes, and when the wind blows, make whirligigs. The breeze is passing through anyway. The old whirligig carvers think it may as well do a little work on its way by.

# Master of the Victrola

The music goes round and round, and —
whoa-ho-ho — it comes out here. These
wonderful machines, made first by Thomas
Edison, gave Americans a chance to hear
something they'd never heard before —
music they weren't making themselves.
Music with neither musicians nor instruments anywhere in sight.

Old Victrolas are prized now, of course.
But what if you get one that doesn't work?
Why, then you must visit Ralph Woodside
at his shop in Georgetown, Massachusetts.
He'll get you back in the groove.

How did he learn to make these
spring-wound wonders good as new again?

---

WOODSIDE  *It was all by guess and by God.*

By guess and by God, for years now, Ralph
Woodside has been restoring what Mr.
Edison thought of as nothing more than an
office device.

WOODSIDE  *Edison never thought it would be a thing for pleasure. You know, for music.*

They really *did* echo all over the world — and still do, thanks to Ralph Woodside.

I have a portable CD player — an amazing machine, to be sure. But try to imagine someone a hundred years from now lovingly polishing one of these.

# A Tune on the Chopping Block

MATT KIRBY *In the Mideast it's called a* haroon. *In Germany it's called a* Hackbrett, *which means literally "chopping block."*

*We* call it the hammer dulcimer, a very old instrument. Matt Kirby of Baldwin, Kansas, is a young master. He makes dulcimers, and makes music on them, too.

Something like the hammer dulcimer has been played in every country and every age, from the marble halls of David and Solomon to the castles of Irish kings and the caravans of Gypsies, and in backwoods camps of this country, too, where the dulcimer was called "the lumberjack piano."

Oh, by the way, Matt Kirby's is the definitive dulcimer — *literally* definitive: look the definition up, and you'll see Matt Kirby with one of his dulcimers.

It's a simple thing, Matt Kirby says: just some strings stretched across a small box. But name another box of any size that endlessly refills itself. Take tens of centuries of music out, and you still haven't emptied it.

# A Cymbal of America

There are many things we are entirely free to show you at the Zildjian Cymbal Works in Norwell, Massachusetts. We can show you the heating of the metal, and the bending, and the shaping, and the cutting to size. We can show you the carving away of whatever is dull to reveal the beautiful glitter inside. We can show you cymbals being tested by an expert cymbal tester — and by a drummer.

But there is one thing we cannot show you. Behind these doors, following a formula that has been kept secret since 1623, alchemists are mixing together the many metals that give Zildjian cymbals their glowing sound. To be let in on that secret, you have to be a family member.

Which Craigie Zildjian is. Granddaughter of the man who brought the business here in 1929, after *twelve generations* in Turkey.

------

ZILDJIAN *That's the Zildjian sound.*

186

After 400 years, the Zildjian sound emphatically survives.

By the way, in Turkish, the name Zildjian means "son of the cymbal maker." Today in America, to jazz drummers and symphony percussionists alike, the old name still rings a bell.

# Turning Back the Clock

In the sunny window of a sunny shop on a sunny street in Chicago, a magician is at work. Oh, I know. The sign said "Tailor and Cleaner," and Joe Silver is both. But he is a magician, too. Do you see the hole in that jacket? Watch. He is making the hole disappear. Joe Silver is a reweaver.

---

SILVER *And I took each thread and matched it together. You've got to have a lot of patience for it. Not everybody could do that, you know.*

I'll say. One by one by one he teases the ends of the broken threads back into the weave of the fabric, as if he were turning the clock back to a time before there *was* a hole. Joe Silver learned to do this as a boy in Poland. He's been doing it now for nearly sixty years.

---

SILVER *Okay, the hole was right in here.*

Now you see it, now you don't.

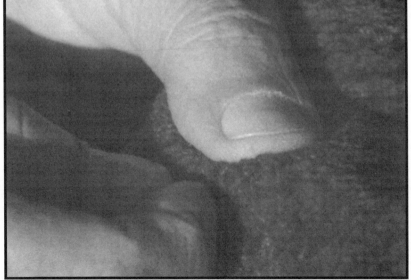

Other things we do and say cannot be undone, more's the pity. But catch your sleeve on a nail, and that bit of bad luck can be undone — by a magician, sitting in the sunny window of a sunny shop on a sunny street in Chicago.

There aren't many reweavers left. The work tries the patience and is hard on the eyes.

Undoing is a dying art.

# Dragonflies, Indeed

You will notice that this woodsman of New York wields no ax. That is because he is not out here to fell a living tree, but to bring dead ones back to life . . . as something else.

Dave Rogers is a sculptor who found years ago while walking in the woods that the fallen trees he was stepping over reminded him of something. What, though? What was it about those shapes that bugged him?

Bugs bugged him, it turned out. Now his spectacular insects travel from botanical garden to botanical garden all over the

country by invitation. The city fathers of West Palm Beach, Florida, thought ants would be nice in their garden. Dave Rogers created some ants for them.

Other sculptors have glorified a puny form of life that uses only two legs, and has but a single pair of eyes and no wings at all. To Dave Rogers, mantises make better subjects than man.

He is a committed man, who long ago learned to let the chips fall where they may.

# A Brush with the Past

Johnny Claypoole tried his hand at many kinds of work, way back when, until his hand found what *it* wanted to do. Now, a lifetime later, Johnny Claypoole is about the last of the hex sign painters of Berks County, Pennsylvania.

There were other artists once, hired by the Pennsylvania Dutch farmers to adorn their barns with star bursts and whirligigs and flowers, one symbol for warding off witches, another for good health and success.

---

CLAYPOOLE *Tulips represent faith — faith, hope, and charity. Your borders are the sea of life, smooth sailing through life.*

Nowadays, of course, people no longer believe in the power of the signs, or do they?

---

CLAYPOOLE *Women in particular say, "I want that," and they read the back of it and they say, "Fertility! Forget it, I've had enough kids." I say, "That's for the crops!"*

193

If it's the latest thing you're looking for, you needn't come to Johnny Claypoole's corner of America. Here in Pennsylvania Dutch country, mostly what you see are — signs of another time.

Johnny Claypoole's distelfinks and mighty oaks and gaudy star bursts may not bring good luck and long life, but they *do* bring pleasure. And what would long life be without that?

# The Strength of Sweet Grass

Rosalee Coaxum of Mount Pleasant, South Carolina, is carrying on an old tradition. It was already an old tradition when her ancestors were brought here as human cargo aboard the slave ships of the eighteenth century.

---

COAXUM *My great-great-grandfather weaved baskets in Africa before he came over here.*

They needed something in which to winnow the rice their masters had set them to cultivating. And so, just as they had done an ocean away when they were free, they gathered what they could find — sweet grass in these parts, and palmetto — to make baskets of.

It's hard to imagine a less substantial growing thing than these slender threads, but braid them together and they are made strong — just as the slender thread of a single life is made strong by being bound up with other lives.

If ever you wonder how a people can have survived slavery, think of the fragile sweet grass of Mount Pleasant becoming the strong and beautiful baskets of Mount Pleasant.

Once upon a time the basket makers of Mount Pleasant used bulrushes for weaving their baskets. I said this was an old tradition. Thousands of years ago the infant Moses was set adrift on the River Nile . . . in a bulrush basket.

# The Fiddler of America

Gene Horner of Rockwood, Tennessee, has been at this since he was a boy. He has made almost three hundred fiddles by now, not to mention various violas and more than a few mandolins.

HORNER  *I had just always wanted to make them.*

He just always wanted to make them. There was no one to teach him how, how to coax a violin out of Tennessee maple and Smoky Mountain spruce. So he taught himself.

HORNER  *It would have been much better and easier if I could have went to school and studied under a really good teacher that knew the correct way and everything.*

No harm done there. Patience is what's needed anyway, the patience slowly to carve, slowly to sand, slowly to see to every detail. Those who know their violins can tell just by looking that these are Horner violins.

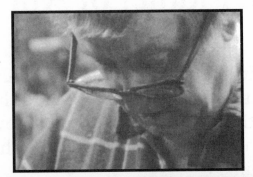

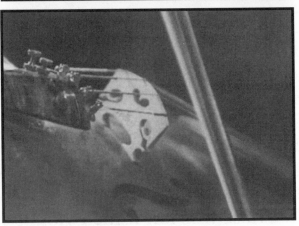

HORNER  *The scroll is just like a signature. There's no two exactly alike. If man ever made anything perfect, it was the fiddle. It has not been improved on in three hundred years.*

I suppose sticklers would say that our fiddle maker couldn't hold a candle to old Antonio Stradivari of Cremona. That's probably true. But I have it on good authority that Stradivari wasn't much at a hoedown.

*American Dreamers*

# With Hope in Hand

Do you remember that poem schoolchildren used to recite? *Under a spreading chestnut tree, the village smithy stands.* Well, the village blacksmith is gone now, mostly. And so, mostly, is the chestnut tree.

Which is why Ron Bockenhauer of West Salem, Wisconsin, has set out to save it.

The chestnut was the greatest tree of the eastern forest. But there came a disastrous blight in 1904. Within thirty years nearly every chestnut was dead and gone. And now these trees brought to Wisconsin as seeds by a settler long ago are among the only ones left. If we're to have American chestnuts in America again, we'll have to depend on devotees like Ron Bockenhauer.

---

BOCKENHAUER *I've kind of fallen in love with the chestnut tree. The chestnut tree is the prettiest tree in the forest!*

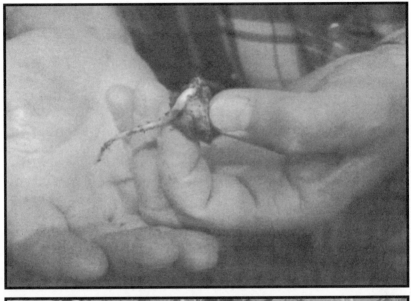

For forty-one years Ron Bockenhauer was an engineer. In his retirement, this old railroad man has become a chestnut man — and a good thing for us that he has.

BOCKENHAUER *That's a chestnut.*

That is a seed of hope you are looking at there. A century ago in the East one tree of every five was a chestnut. Now, in all this country, there may be fifty fully grown chestnut trees.

But where there is life, there is hope.

# Trombone Shorty

Children always learn the language of the place in which they live. Troy Andrews lives in New Orleans. The language here is music.

"Trombone Shorty," he is called. The "Shorty" part you understand; he is ten years old. He is *Trombone* Shorty" because that was the instrument he used to play around with. Now it's the tuba. And now he doesn't play around. He *plays*.

With the Williams boys — Sam and Duane — on drums, Shorty's older brother James on trumpet, and a friend on trombone, the band warms up while waiting for the sun to set. They walk through Louis Armstrong Park to Jackson Square in the French Quarter.

Ask Trombone Shorty why he does this.

SHORTY  *I like jazz.*

Ask for whom he does it.

SHORTY  *Myself.*

208

No mention of money, nor of fame. The music is all that matters.

New Orleans is a city of the senses. But even if you were deprived of some of them, you'd still know where you were, as long as you could hear.

A couple of years ago I heard the grand old man of New Orleans jazz, Percy Humphrey, still playing powerful horn in his nineties. We wish Trombone Shorty the same staying power.

# Play Ball!

Does that jacket say three-quarters of a century of softball experience? Really?

---

HARRY SHIRONAKA  *My name is Harry Shironaka. I'll be eighty-five in twenty days.*

---

JOHN ELIAS  *John Elias, eighty-four.*

---

OTHER PLAYER  *Wacko! He's probably only seventy-five. We get a lot of those kids around here.*

These Florida gentlemen call themselves the Kids and the Kubs. To play in their league you have to be seventy-five to be a rookie.

---

PAT ROWLEY  *I'm Pat Rowley. I'm eighty-five years old.*

---

OTHER PLAYER  *They follow instructions — the ones that can hear!*

OTHER PLAYER  *Oh geez! I keep forgetting to look.*

WALT PAULEY  *I'm Walt Pauley, seventy-seven years old. My batting average, let's see, about .782.*

OTHER PLAYER  *Hey, do we have batting averages?*

PAULEY  *Yeah — .225.*

OTHER PLAYER  *Did they tell you this is a procedure we go through? Almost every day: white pants and shirts and black bow ties.*

OTHER PLAYER  *At least the tie isn't wrinkled like we are!*

UMPIRE  *All right, gentlemen, play ball!*

Don't tell these guys that it's only a game. It's life to them. And they're living.

# And Then the Curtain Fell

---

BOB PARRISH   *"My darling, I am dreaming . . ."*

That is quite a voice Bob Parrish has. So said the very famous opera teacher who took him on as a student when he was young. There followed recordings and performances and applause.

But Bob Parrish's wife died, alas, and he had children to raise. So the farm boy who was poised to become an opera singer returned to the farm. A life on the land is an uncertain one, but less uncertain than a life on the stage.

Is this a sad story? Mostly, no, it isn't.

---

PARRISH   *I love the farm. It's my way of life.*

Fame eluded him, but *not* success. In Stitzer, Wisconsin, Bob Parrish made a life for his family, and filled that life with music. He is a success.

PARRISH  *"And I'll soon give you ten thousand more."*

Not ten thousand more like Bob Parrish. Of this sort of stouthearted man, there is only one.

"How're you going to keep 'em down on the farm?" was the question people used to ask. The answer is, pretty often life will see to that.

But Bob Parrish, farmer, is still a good singer. And something more. He's a good man.

# By the Billion

The tall timbers of Maine have been turned into many things: spars and masts for sailing ships, roof beams, pilings for piers and bridges. And, for a century and a half, into something smaller, too.

Toothpicks, millions a day, billions a year, all out of this place: Forster's, named for the company's founder, who went traveling to Brazil in the 1850s and saw the Indians there using whittled bits of wood to clean their teeth. Eureka, he thought. Charles Forster had a plan, as Forster's general manager Rich Campbell can tell us.

CAMPBELL *He hired a group of debonair young men from Harvard University to go to the finest restaurants in Boston, and after their meal, the young men would ask the maître d' for a toothpick.*

When told, of course, that there were no toothpicks, the young men made a fuss. Restaurants took to laying in supplies of toothpicks.

They mostly come from the white birches of Maine. And one cord, by the way, yields three million toothpicks.

It is an American success story, of course, if a little backward. Charles Forster looked up at a towering tree, and dared to think small.

# Flowers That Fly

Here you have Cliff Ross of Santa Fe, New Mexico, helping some children plan a birthday party for a friend of theirs. Friend of yours, too.

------

ROSS *We started going around and asking kids if they would like to have a birthday party for the Earth.*

And what to get the Earth for its birthday?

------

ROSS *One little guy said, "I think we should all take our shoes off on that day, because can you imagine how the Earth must feel with all of us walking on it?"*

But Cliff Ross and other teachers around the country settled on something else. Earth Day is the day they chose as the birthday of our planet. And here is what they chose to give the planet.

------

CHILD *Butterflies.*

This year, out of cocoons in classrooms everywhere, there came hundreds of thousands of gifts for the planet Earth. It makes sense. If we can seed the soil, why not the sky? Think of Cliff Ross as a Johnny Appleseed of the air. This is a kind of gardening, after all. What are these delicate creatures but flowers that fly?

If Cliff Ross and the Earth's Birthday Project have their way, a million school children of America will be releasing butterflies into the air by the year 2000, all on the same day!

The Earth *has* seemed a little grumpy in the last century or so. That ought to cheer it up.

# A Gift of Wisdom

This is the story of a gift Martha Freeman was given years ago as a child here beside the Sheepscot River of Maine. The gift came from a friend of her grandmother's, who was also summering nearby. Rachel Carson was the friend.

---

FREEMAN *At low tide there's a lot of uncovered crevices in the rocks where water forms, and all kinds of little sea creatures live. More than anything she wanted us to see the beauty, to understand that starfish, sea urchins, mussels, clams, are living beings just like we are, and to notice how each one was its own individual. This place means an incredible amount to me.*

The gift Rachel Carson gave Martha Freeman, she gave the world as well, in books that taught us all how fragile nature is. What was true here, Rachel Carson realized, was true all over the planet. There is life underfoot wherever you step — so watch where you step.

Rachel Carson wrote this splendid book of hers, *The Sea Around Us*, after looking down into a tidal pool. She showed Martha Freeman how important that place was — and then, she showed all the rest of us.

# His Big Small World

This is not Gulliver in the land of the Lilliputians. Bruce Zaccagnino figured people would pay to see what he could do. He had outgrown his basement by then. He had outgrown many basements. So he had a building built — Northlands — in Flemington, New Jersey, inside which he created a fifty-thousand-square-foot America in miniature, from the mountains to the prairies to the oceans — well, the rivers — white with foam.

The children who come here are especially wide-eyed, of course, and why wouldn't they be? They've spent all their time so far looking *up* at the world. Here's a world they can look *down* at.

More than a hundred model trains crisscross this landscape. But do not call it a model train layout. Bruce Zaccagnino considers himself an artist.

And do you wonder how his wonderland was made?

ZACCAGNINO *It's piece by piece, you know.*

Of course. Piece by piece. By piece. By piece.

We all live in our own little worlds. But Bruce Zaccagnino's little world *isn't* little. Even so, he plans to expand, though all he is willing to say about his new landscape is that it will be really spectacular.

Give him this: for a man who works small, he thinks big.

# The Call of the Wild

That is not a wolf you are hearing. That is a wolf photographer.

Jim Brandenburg of Minnesota is this country's preeminent photographer of wolves. You will notice, however, that he doesn't have a camera with him at the moment. That is because he is not here to take pictures.

---

BRANDENBURG *I'd almost rather hear the wolves than see them, because that howl is so enchanting and so primal. Howling is very serious business to a wolf.*

Jim Brandenburg has qualms about doing this at all. Howling is serious business to him, too. And he tries not to impose too often on the animals that have become — as much as wild animals can — his friends.

Still and all, if he's not heard their wonderful voices for a long time . . .

**BRANDENBURG** *Every once in a while you need a fix.*

He howls, and sometimes from out in the distance a wolf howls back.

There are a few sounds in nature that you not only hear, but also feel, as an actual thrill in the blood. The call of the loon is like that, and the bugle of the elk, and the howl of the wolf in the woods of Minnesota. Hear it, and you half think it's *you* they're calling to come and join the pack. Hear it again, and you half think you just might.

*American Sights*

# Snow Geese

Every year, down from the tundra of the north come the snow geese. They come to the Klamath Basin first, on the Oregon-California border. Then they fly south to Central California.

They come by the hundreds of thousands. There are no words for this western migration. Sometimes there are more birds than sky. I think it's one of the great, heart-stopping sights of the world.

It's the same to the left of what I'm showing you, the same again to the right, and the same behind us. There is no lens big enough to take this all in.

In the air nowadays are television pictures, streams of data, cellular chat. I thought you might like to be reminded what the air is really for. It's for them.

Really, the pictures do not do it justice. You have to stand there, as the only creature left behind on the ground after the great rising up of everything else in sight. With the wind of so many wings still on your face, you suddenly know very well what it means to be *earthbound*.

# The Valley of the Eagles

We are near the town of Haines, Alaska, in what is called the Valley of the Eagles. It is called that for good reason. This is where the eagles gather, in season. By ones and twos. By threes and fours. By sixes and sevens.

The day we visited, there were 1,445 bald eagles in this one river valley, which is to say more feathered majesty per mile here than anywhere else on earth. Majesty and strength.

Ask ranger Bill Zack, who once had to subdue an injured bald eagle to tend to it.

---

ZACK  *When I threw the blanket over it, it actually lifted me up off the snow.*

They can lift you right off the ground. But keep your distance, and eagles will lift your *spirit* off the ground instead. To look at a bald eagle is to soar a little yourself.

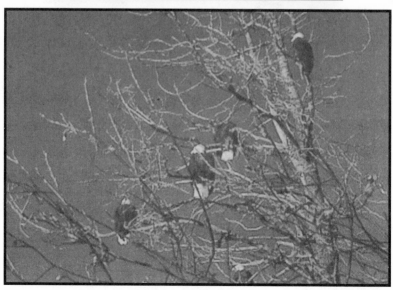

I expect you know that Ben Franklin thought the turkey, not the eagle, ought to be the symbol of this country.

Ben Franklin had thousands of good ideas — and at least one bad one.

# Giants in the Earth

You know the words of the book of Genesis: "There were giants in the earth in those days." Well, in these days, too, there are giants in the earth.

There are the sequoias of California. Some of these trees have been growing here for three thousand years. The sequoias are the largest living things on earth.

Think about it. When buildings were built, in the first years of this century, that were ten and twenty and then thirty stories high, the world was stunned and gave them a new name — skyscrapers. By then, at more than three hundred feet tall, these trees had been scraping the sky for many hundreds of years.

Look not *up* but *at* them, and you can see their age. This might be the skin of Father Time himself, lost in a dream of the dawn of the world.

They have been called sequoias only for the last little bit of their very long lives, after Chief Sequoyah of the Cherokees, who died in 1843. What they were called in the

twenty or twenty-five centuries before Sequoyah was born, while they were growing up there in California, I don't know. Perhaps no tiny human being had the temerity to *give* them a name, until our day.

# In the Shallows

The sights to see at Florida's Crystal River Wildlife Refuge are down here. These are manatees. They come to Crystal River for the winter warmth of the underwater springs, and because elsewhere — and here, too — their habitat is dwindling. Ask refuge manager Ted Ondler about the outlook for the manatees.

ONDLER *I think they are going to have a real precarious existence through this next century. They're barely holding their own right now.*

God bless the manatees, which haven't an aggressive bone in their bodies. Not many bones of any kind, to judge by the looks of them. They are sweet and slow and guileless. And easily harmed by two things they do not know enough to get out of the way of: boat propellers and progress.

Sailors of old saw slow-moving gray shadows in the shoals. Some say that's how the myth of the mermaid was born. Now manatees may become as rare as mermaids.

Beasts of the field have claws and teeth; birds of the air have talons and speed. We have our wits and our weapons. Manatees have no defense at all. They trust to luck in this world. Good luck to them.

# Windblown Seeds

Here is some beauty for you from the Hill Country of Texas: spectacular fields of bluebonnets spring up wherever you look. What painter could manage such scenes as this? Or manage the red mixed in with the blue here and there? Or manage that piercing yellow? It would make the brush shake in your hand.

This beauty was not painted, or planted. The earth managed all this pretty much by itself. The wind did this work, spreading the seeds of wildflowers far and wide.

We worry about the damage we've done by trampling the surface of the earth. But look here. Almost as soon as we walk away, the bluebonnets grow bold.

When our trespass is over, the wind comes, bringing flowers.

Lady Bird Johnson, that treasure of Texas, is a famous defender and planter of the wildflowers of her state. But the wind takes over from her, too.

Beauty only needs the rest of us to leave it be.

# Key Deer

Whatever grows out of the dry soil of the Florida Keys is fragile and slender and delicate. That goes for the wildlife, too.

These are miniature deer, found nowhere else on earth but in the lower Keys of Florida. There came a glacier long ago to cut the Keys off from the mainland. The Key deer, isolated from their mainland cousins, adapted to island life by learning to drink brackish water and by eating less. That's why they're so small. Small in number, too. Listen to ranger Barry Stiglitz:

STIGLITZ *Twenty years ago, on Big Pine Key, which really has the core of the Key deer herd, there were probably four hundred Key deer. And the human population was under a thousand. And in the last twenty years or so, we've seen the human population go up to almost five thousand and the deer population go down.*

The little deer barely look up now when the cars pass. Every year some of their lives are taken by speeding cars. What if the Key deer are wiped out?

STIGLITZ *Whether I see them or not, to know that they're there means something to me.*

They have been in the Keys all along. *We* are the newcomers.

The little Key deer have learned to make do with less. How much less than less can they learn to make do with?

# Among the Swans

This is Lake Mattamuskeet on the coast of North Carolina, where the tundra swans rest at last after their long flight from the Arctic. Some come from Siberia, thousands of miles away, and have done so for thousands of years. They are beautiful to see.

The great poet of Ireland, William Butler Yeats, wrote these lines in "The Wild Swans at Coole":

> *The trees are in their autumn beauty,*
> *The woodland paths are dry,*
> *Under the October twilight the water*
> *Mirrors a still sky;*
> *Upon the brimming water among*
> *   the stones*
> *Are nine-and-fifty swans.*
>
> *The nineteenth autumn has come*
> *   upon me*
> *Since I first made my count;*
> *I saw, before I had well finished,*
> *All suddenly mount*

And scatter wheeling in great
  broken rings
Upon their clamorous wings.

I have looked upon those brilliant
  creatures,
And now my heart is sore.
All's changed since I, hearing at
  twilight,
The first time on this shore,
The bell-beat of their wings
  above my head,
Trod with a lighter tread.

Unwearied still, lover by lover,
They paddle in the cold
Companionable streams or climb
  the air;
Their hearts have not grown old;
Passion or conquest, wander
  where they will,
Attend upon them still.

But now they drift on the still water,
Mysterious, beautiful;
Among what rushes will they build,
By what lake's edge or pool
Delight men's eyes when I
  awake some day
To find they have flown away?

Spring is coming. They're about to fly away. Thousands of miles away. North, toward home.

You may remember what happened after Zeus, the greatest of all the Olympian gods of Greece, fell in love with a mortal woman. He figured he wouldn't stand a chance with her as just a god, so he turned himself into — a swan.

# A World of Ice

It's hot outside, so we've come up here for a cool drink. And for some ice. There is a world of ice in Alaska.

This world, the Mendenhall Glacier, largest of the thirty-eight glaciers of the two-thousand-square-mile Juneau Ice Field. The Mendenhall is a river, really, forever clenched in a monumental fist, in peaks and rills and caps, and billowing sails, all enormous, all of ice.

The shapes look blue here and there. The ice is so densely compacted that, of all the wavelengths of light, only the blue waves escape.

The glacier *does* move, at the pace we call — glacial. And over time — millions of years of time — it has been the author of the landscape here, carving and parting and piling up, out of the way, whatever may have been *in* the way — even the mountains.

"Some say the world will end in fire," the poet wrote. "Some say in ice." And then the poet himself came down on the side of fire.

But I don't believe Robert Frost ever saw the Mendenhall Glacier, where the world, if not ended, has at least paused now for a very long while.

# The Unstoppable Sand

If the sea were not of water, but of sand, this is what it would look like. These are the gypsum dunes of White Sands, New Mexico, slowly, endlessly leapfrogging one another, cresting and collapsing, heaped up and crumbling down.

The movement never stops here, any more than the ocean's movement stops. The dunes creep and crawl and shift; the sand shrugs and slumps and is raked and combed by the wind — and driven on by the wind, always driven on, to cover everything. The dunes are unstoppable.

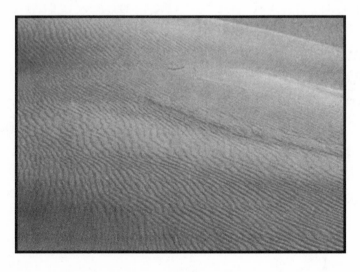

What could possibly live here? The occasional yucca. A plant called a skunkbush. A bit of a bug. Otherwise, these dunes largely are barren. Of course they are. We can live *with* the sands of time, but we cannot live *on* them.

On the sixteenth of July, 1945, at five-thirty in the morning, the first atomic bomb was detonated a few miles away near Alamogordo. The scientists and their instruments of death are long gone. The land belongs again to the shifting sands.

# Bundles of Blooms

GROWER *I've seen these fields completely yellow.*

Yellow? What sort of crop would make a field yellow? This sort — a crop of daffodils.

The daffodils are all gone by for the year, of course. But what is the point of keeping a kind of a family album of the country if you can't turn the pages backwards now and then. And there isn't a prettier page to turn back to than this one.

Wheat and corn are important crops, no question about that. But this daffodil farm in Virginia provides nourishment, too — for the soul. And it is portable beauty that is grown in these fields: by the handful at first, and then the armful, beauty goes forth in bundles of blooms.

How else to set hope down, bright yellow hope, on distant desks and tabletops all over the country? Everything changes in our dim rooms and offices when the daffodils arrive. They amount to a kind of bulletin in a vase,

a news flash to say: things are looking up, so we can, too.

The center of a daffodil is called the trumpet. Of course it is. What else would a messenger have but a trumpet?

# Stone New Yorkers

Floridians don't go to the beach, and Manhattanites don't look up. But they *should*. Whether they know it or not, the people of the city of New York have friends in high places.

There are gargoyles on the cathedrals of New York. And on its cathedrals of commerce. And stone caricatures on the apartment buildings of New York: raffish cartoon portraits of one another by long-gone master masons.

Gargoyles are descendants of the downspouts of the Middle Ages, designed to gush rainwater. New York City Parks Commissioner Henry Stern likes to gush about the gargoyles.

---

STERN  *The gargoyle is an absolutely fascinating piece of architectural ornamentation. Here is a gargoyle who appears to be wrapped in thought.*

They are made fierce in order to ward off evil spirits. And for another reason, too.

STERN  *They were also a warning of what might happen to you in the next world if you didn't behave yourself in this one.*

New York would be the place for such a warning. There are saints here, yes. But — sinners, too.

Gargoyles are monstrous and grotesque and repugnant. At least the good ones are.

# Brief Beauty

May we give you a summertime gift of spring? These are the cherry blossoms of Washington, D.C. No beauty is more fleeting than these blooms. They come and go all in a matter of days. They leave beautiful memories.

The chief horticulturist for the National Park Service, Robert Defeo, tends these gifts to America from Japan.

------

DEFEO *In Japan the cherry tree is a symbol of life, because the blossom of the cherry tree is very short-lived — short, but sweet.*

They are surprising as life, too. All of a sudden, out of a bare branch comes a green fuse, and then the fuse bursts to become a translucent pink flower, and then very soon the flower falls.

These are pictures of the past, yes, but of the future, too: come another spring, it will all happen again, fuse and flower and fall.

Of the three thousand or so cherry trees that came to this country from Japan in 1912,

a hundred and fifty still are there in Washington, and still are blooming.

It's only a brief blaze of beauty, but one that we remember all year.

# American Heirlooms

# Heavenly Windows, Hellish Hate

We have come to this fine old church of Buffalo, New York, to tell you the story of a rivalry.

This is a window by John La Farge. And *this* is a window by Louis Comfort Tiffany. Tiffany and La Farge despised each other.

It was La Farge who dreamed up the first real advance in stained glass since the Middle Ages, an advance that made his windows radiant and luminous. La Farge patented his opalescent glass process in 1880, but by then he had already explained it to Louis Tiffany, who tried it for himself, and liked it, and went right on using it. La Farge said Tiffany stole the process. There was a lawsuit. There was bitterness. There was lifelong hatred.

Who won the feud? Buffalo's Trinity Church did. It has some of the most achingly beautiful stained-glass windows to be found anywhere in the world.

La Farge displayed his most magnificent

window in Paris. The French government wanted to buy it, but La Farge sent it home to Buffalo. Of course he did — who do you think would have filled the space had La Farge left it vacant?

# Hoppin' John

LUCILLE GRANT *You make your peas first, and then put in all your seasonings. And then I add my rice to it.*

In her kitchen in the low country of South Carolina, Ms. Lucille Grant is cooking rice and black-eyed peas, flavored by salt pork and honored by ancient tradition. It's a pot of good luck is what it is: Hoppin' John.

GRANT *If you don't have Hoppin' John in your house, and collard greens, it just ain't New Year's to you.*

Well, it depends on where you live. In Boston, they favor oyster stew on New Year's Day. In Milwaukee, pickled herring, and so on across the country. This is a very tasty national disagreement.

GRANT *The way I make Hoppin' John is the way my mother used to make it.*

It's the way my mother made it, too — rice and field peas and fatback on January first for good luck through the year. And a shiny dime in the pot. Whoever got the dime was in for the best luck of all. We've had our good luck already. Pleased to make your acquaintance, Ms. Grant.

No, we're not all fast food from coast to coast. We're not the same. Go into the right kitchen, lift the lid of a pot, and you can still tell about where you are in this country.

If you're looking for the spirit of a place, head for the stove.

# Let There Be Light

This is *not* the original Livermore, California, firehouse. But this *is* the original Livermore, California, firehouse *lightbulb*. This bulb has been burning in the Livermore firehouse ever since it was first turned on. It was first turned on in 1901. The record books agree. This is the longest-burning lightbulb in the world.

Think of it. Behind that handblown glass, those thick carbide filaments have been glowing for ninety-six years. From the time of Teddy Roosevelt, to our time. From horse-drawn hose carts to long yellow trucks. From a couple of years before Kitty Hawk to a generation after man's landing on the moon.

I know. You skeptics are saying that the light must have been turned off when it was brought here from the old firehouse in 1978. And you're right. On moving day, it *was* turned off — for twenty-three minutes.

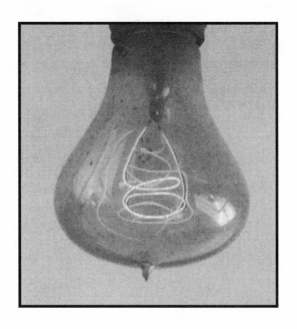

If Livermore, California, does not already have a town song to call its own, I suggest the one that goes, "This little light of mine, I'm gonna let it shine."

If you are wondering where you can get a bulb that might last a century or so — you can't. That one was made by the Shelby Electric Company, which went out of business long ago. Of course it did. No one ever had to order a second lightbulb from Shelby Electric.

# America's Sunrise

Here is something I can tell you for a fact. No matter when the sun comes up in your part of the country, it comes up in *this* part of the country first. This is Guam. No bit of America is farther from the rest of America than Guam is. About the time banks are closing in New York on Friday, people here are sitting down to Saturday's breakfast. Guam, west of the International Date Line, is nearer tomorrow than today.

Ferdinand Magellan, the great Portuguese circumnavigator, was the first European to see this island. Spain colonized Guam, and ceded it to us following the Spanish-American War of 1898. So for pretty nearly a century now, this has been where America's day begins.

If it seems odd that this country should have so faraway a possession, consider how we got it. The American battleship *Maine* was sunk in a harbor of Cuba. Teddy Roosevelt charged up a hill in Puerto Rico. There were naval battles in the Philippines, after which a peace treaty was signed in

Paris. And there, a tiny island of the Pacific, belonging to defeated Spain, came to be the most distant shore of the United States of America.

# The Weight of Progress

Do you know what that building is? It's a scale. The whole building is a scale. That is the 1850 Weighlock Building of Syracuse, New York, the last of the float-in scales where tolls were collected by weight on the Erie Canal.

How did it work? Ask Canal Museum curator Mark Koziol.

---

KOZIOL *The boats would come in through the lock system, and the two lock doors would then close, and the water would drain out of the canal and go into a creek. And as the boat started to sink down into the water, it would be caught by the scale.*

Then came the calculations down at the weighmaster's office: a penny a pound for corn, so much for salt and whiskey and rum, so much for coal and for manufactured goods. The average toll per boat was about a hundred dollars. Millions of dollars were collected, keg by keg and crate by crate, before the country outgrew the canal.

If you think your local toll booth slows you down, consider this. One summer season in the last century twenty thousand boats floated through Syracuse, and the passengers had to get off every one so that it could be weighed.

# The Devil's Rope

VAL FERRIN  *At one time in this country you didn't have to stop for anything. You could go through any man's property, any man's ranch, unless he started shooting.*

It is as Val Ferrin says — cattlemen and their herds *could* go wherever they wanted in the West. Then came barbed wire, which is collected and traded as a historical artifact here in La Crosse, Kansas.

EUGENE HENRY WALKER  *Once they put in the barbed wire, then it tamed them boys down.*

Tell us, Mr. Walker, how long have you been collecting barbed wire?

WALKER  *Well, I started in 1948.*

And now you have *how* many kinds?

WALKER  *Eighteen hundred and thirty-nine.*

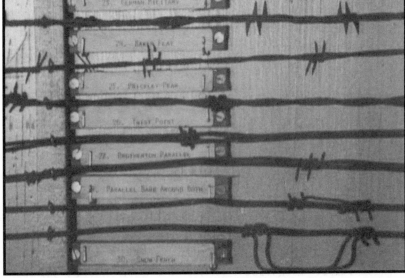

"The Devil's Rope" is what it was called when it was invented in the 1860s. That was when the fence posts began to appear, with a second horizon — a *wire* horizon — strung between them.

As much as the telegraph, this wire also carried a message over great distances. The message was: the West is wilderness no longer.

"This land is your land," the great old folk song says. The modern rancher says, "Oh, no, I put this barbed-wire fence up. This land is *mine*."

# Ink in the Blood

And now the news, picked out letter by letter and set in hot metal on a Linotype machine by Marie Coombs, who has been editor of the Saguache, Colorado, *Crescent* for sixty-two years. Her father was editor before her.

Papers aren't printed this way anymore, but *this* one *is*. Four pages a week, every week since 1917. Four pages of good news. There's no reason to print the other kind.

---

COOMBS  *In a small town everybody knows what you're doing, anyway.*

*When people come in, they'll say, "I need the* Crescent. *" That kind of puts it in a nutshell, I think.*

They *need* the *Crescent* — to gather 'round. It's a four-page mirror they look into every week, polished by Marie Coombs.

May I tell you something? These scenes make my heart beat faster. I can run a linotype machine. It's become about the most useless skill in the world, nearly everywhere but here.

Some of the *Crescent*'s stories are too long for one edition and have to be published serially. So down there at the bottom of many a page, more often than not, you will find what might be the *real* motto of Marie Coombs: *To be continued.*

We hope so.

# Elephants of the Harbor

This is an open letter to the tugboat captains of New York Harbor: I envy you, and I always have been in love with your boats.

They are all engine, just barely surrounded by hull. What tugs do in the harbors of the world is what elephants do in the jungles of the world. No matter what the weight, up they come, steady and undaunted, to put their great heads against it, resolved absolutely that the contest will end only when the obstacle in front of them has given way.

Push and strain and urge, until the weight moves, and keeps on moving. In the jungle, by now, a tree would have fallen. Here, a ship is docked.

Back there are the twin towers of the World Trade Center. Without these elephants of the harbor, and the drivers who straddle their great necks, there wouldn't be very much world trade.

Tugboats mostly *don't* tug anymore. They nudge from the side or push from the back. But it would not be respectful enough to call them *push* boats. And tugboats *do* deserve respect.

# The Last of Jesse James

GARY CHILCOTE  *It was a warm morning, and the front door was open.*

It's the third of April, 1882, that historian Gary Chilcote is talking about.

CHILCOTE  *Bob and Charles Ford were gang members, and they were seated right over here on this divan. They noticed that Jesse took off his guns and placed them on the divan, and climbed on a chair over here across the room to straighten this picture. And that was the chance they had been waiting for. They drew their guns, and Bob fired, and the bullet came in behind Jesse's right ear.*

Exit Jesse James. But why was such a man a legend even then?

CHILCOTE *Jesse was the first outlaw in the American West. He came along right after the Civil War. And he did things that a lot of people rather admired secretly. The James gang robbed trains and they robbed banks, and the people didn't like either one of them. The railroads had the old "public be damned" attitude, and the bankers were hard to deal with after the war. So they really didn't feel too sorry for the victims.*

Die a law-abiding citizen and you may be remembered for a time. Die a desperado and you will be remembered for *all* time. Gary Chilcote tells us there are Jesse James fan clubs all over Europe — and in Japan.

It seems the third of April, 1882, was an American Moment to remember.

# Wind Your Bobbin

Sewing was done by hand on this earth for thousands of years — after which the next step forward was sewing by foot: treadle sewing machines came in before the Civil War.

Many are still coming into the shop of Steven and Cathy Racine in Charlton, Massachusetts.

They both do the repairs, by the way.

---

CATHY RACINE *When I was a little girl, I had my own toolbox; I had my own goggles so I could work on my father's lathe.*

By training, Cathy Racine is a teacher of autistic children. She finds parallels in her two lines of work.

---

RACINE *Sewing machine repair has a start and a finish, and the finish is always a working machine, so it was a very, very important part of my life during my teaching career.*

And this teacher *learned* something, too, working with her hands.

RACINE *If you work on machines from the 1860s to the 1880s, you have worked on machines that account for the historical development of a stitch being made. And they did it in 1860 just as well as they do it in 1997. So you know, the old machines are just so beautifully made, and they do the exact same thing.*

Well, that's our story. I guess it is literally a story about a stitch in time.

# Good Things Come in Big Boxes Too

Villa Park, Illinois, is a town of straight streets and very homey-looking homes, many of which came by mail.

There were *hundreds* of models of houses to choose from in the Sears catalogue, once upon a time — from modest to magnificent. The names were nice, too: the Magnolia, the Preston, the Alhambra. And everything was included, all the plumbing and electrical fixtures and all.

This five-room Crescent was mail-ordered from Sears. Seldom, said the ad, do you find a more inviting entrance than we provide for this house.

---

BOB STRAIT *Oh, the front porch was a gathering place, a neighborly place.*

Bob Strait's father took possession of the many boxes in which his Crescent came in 1919, and then he followed the directions.

STRAIT  *It was a wonderful home to grow up in.*

Sears stopped selling houses by mail in the 1940s, but a lot of them still are around, not looking at all as if they had arrived in pieces. Go up into your attic and take a look. If your rafters are numbered, *yours* may be a catalogue house.

It's nothing remarkable these days to have packages arrive on your doorstep, but there on your doorstep once upon a time might have been a package containing — your doorstep, next to other packages containing the rest of your house. And we call *this* an age of wonders!

# The Towers Atop the Towers of New York

WALLACE ROSENWACH *You look at the sky-line and you say, "That's our skyline. We helped create it."*

That is true, but Wallace Rosenwach is not an architect. He is a cooper. The barrels he makes are very big ones. His family has been doing this work for more than a century.

ROSENWACH *My grandfather bought the business from the widow of the man he worked for in 1896 for fifty-five dollars.*

By law every Manhattan building of seven stories or more must have on its roof a big water barrel on stilts to supply sprinklers that will begin to dampen whatever is burning while the firefighters are still on their way. The great city decided long ago to depend on gravity in the first minutes of such emergencies — and to depend on Rosenwach water tanks.

ROSENWACH *Half the tanks that my father put up in the twenties are still up there. Now that's a long time!*

So atop the modern city that taught the world what modern cities ought to be, there they are, the hoops and staves of the Middle Ages. Whoever thought the old art of the barrel maker would rise to such heights?

In other places you have to dig down to find the past. In New York City to find the past you have to go up. New York City is an odd place.

# Scratched in the Landscape

Go into the canyon and mesa country of central New Mexico, and you think at first, There *never* have been human beings here. But that is wrong.

Centuries ago, and tens of centuries ago, the ancestors of the Pueblo people stood before these stones to scratch messages into them. What the messages meant no one can say for certain now. There are faces here, and figures. Birds, and snakes. Animals. And geometric designs.

Some of these markings were here before Columbus came to the New World, or Christ to the Old World. The Pueblo were here, chipping at these stones, when Plato was walking in his garden in Greece.

We say of something about which we may change our minds, "Well, it isn't chiseled in stone." Here in New Mexico, you can see why we say that: Once a thing *is* chiseled in stone, it is there for the ages.

"Petroglyphs" is what the pictures are called. There are thousands of them all over America. We don't know what the pictures were *meant* to tell us, but they *do* tell us one thing quite clearly: This is a young country, yes — but an old land.

*American Ways*

# Skipping Stones

This is about as much fun as I remember ever having when I was a kid — skipping stones. I practiced and got good at it. Twelve or thirteen skips was pretty good. I remember searching the shore for a certain round, smooth stone that felt just about perfect — but wasn't, as it turned out. But there was always another stone, and another chance at a personal best.

---

YOUNG BOY  *I got three skips.*

Who can say why this is so satisfying? It just is. "To sink like a stone" is the expression. But, if you do it right, it *doesn't* sink. Not right away. It hops and leaps and sails and pit-a-pats across the water.

I was sure back then that the next stone would be better. And the one after that better still. Stone-skippers have to be eternal optimists.

You can think deep thoughts while you're skipping stones, if you like. Or you can just make the stones plink and fly.

An idle moment is an American Moment, too.

# The Ferry at Los Ebanos

People have been crossing the Rio Grande at Los Ebanos at least since the 1700s — on horseback or on foot. Or, in the second half of this century, *this* way — by means of a hand-powered ferry.

All day long, back and forth, from Mexico on one bank to Texas on the other, the ferrymen pull a few cars and a few pedestrians at a time. The ferry is licensed by the government, but has been privately owned all along by the family that opened it in 1950.

The crossing takes minutes, and costs one quarter per person, six quarters per car.

In the government's official classification scheme, Los Ebanos is a "Class A" port of entry — same as Houston is, same as New York.

But Los Ebanos is *not* the same as those places at all. Come into the country here, *this* way, and you learn the lesson right off: to be an American, you have to pull your own weight. But you have to be willing to help pull the weight of others, too.

There is talk that a bridge may be built at Los Ebanos. But the talk is nearly as old as the ferry is. And I, for one, hope it remains talk. I'm always on the lookout, you know, for a slower way to go. I think the ferry at Los Ebanos qualifies nicely.

# The Blessing of the Fleet

The time has come in Bayou La Batre, Alabama, to take a number and form a line — of fishing boats to be blessed.

It's a gaudy show every year, and a grand occasion. But the blessing of the fleet is more than that.

---

FISHERMAN *We had a terrible season last year, and maybe God will hear us this year if we pray loud enough.*

It is not for their livings only that they pray. They pray for their lives. After all, the sea can do worse than withhold its bounty.

So raise up your voice, Abbot Clark. Much depends on your being heard.

---

ABBOT CLARK *As we implore God's protection for all who put out to sea, bring them back with glad hearts to their own shores and homes.*

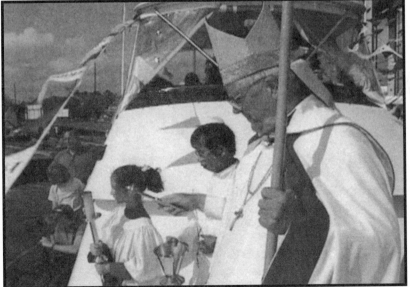

The boats and the clothing would have been different on the Sea of Galilee. But the faces of the fishermen surely were the same. And the *prayers* of the fishermen surely were the same: Let the sea be generous. Let the sea be merciful.

They are shrimpers mostly, there in Bayou La Batre. Next time you're tempted to scowl at the prices on the menu, think about those who go and get your feast for you out of the Gulf, and what the cost of that feast may be to *them*.

# A Rite of Spring

For days now on his ranch in McKinney, Texas, there has been nothing much for Bill Stokes to do but prepare and fret and wait. He and his beautiful Arabian mare both know the moment is near. Bill Stokes is waiting for something he has seen often by now, but which stuns him, which stuns anyone, every time it happens.

He is waiting for this.

After months of floating in the dark without knowledge that it *has* legs, out the foal comes to extend the slender limbs there never has been room to extend before, so that they will accept the weight the foal does not yet know it has.

Not yet. Not quite yet. After just a few more tries, though, and a little rest, it will happen.

It *has* happened. The foal's age still must be reckoned by the clock, but Bill Stokes knows everything is going to be all right now. The foal seems to know it, too.

A human baby spends a good year learning how to stand. In a few hours, a

horse stands, and walks, and runs. Look at
one, newborn or full grown, at full gallop,
and you have to think — whatever gave us
the temerity to make a servant of that?

# Miss Indian World

These beauty pageant finalists *are* beautiful; you can see that for yourself. But they are here in Albuquerque to be judged on something you *cannot* see. This is a *spiritual* beauty contest, really.

Every year at the great powwow called the Gathering of Nations, a new Miss Indian World is crowned. What the winner must show is more than a pretty form. She must show a deep knowledge of the ways of her people.

These contestants have learned how to find healing plants in the hills, and how to read the lessons of the earth underfoot. They have learned to sing their people's songs, and tell their people's tales. They have learned what their elders have to teach. The winner will represent an ancient wisdom.

---

MISS INDIAN WORLD  *To all these beautiful young ladies, I congratulate you all.*

We congratulate you all, too.

This year's Miss Indian World, Shayai Lucero of New Mexico, gets no convertible car or recording contract or trip to a theme park. For the deep respect she has shown her people, she gets — the deep respect of her people. Not a small prize.

# Of Horse and Man

Does it take a tough man to break a colt? Actually, no. It takes a *gentle* man. Ask Vic Ogle.

---

OGLE *The more peaceful you can make it, the better off you are. If you make it a fight, you're going to lose.*

These colts of Colorado aren't being *broken* really, on the ranch of Wade Collins, he of the splendid mustache: they are being befriended and taught.

---

COLLINS *These horses will learn in a year and be fairly well-finished riding horses. But we've got to go to school for twelve years just to get through high school, and we're not finished yet. I guess we ain't quite as smart!*

What happens in the movies in a blur of sound and fury takes months in real life, and fury can have no part in it. Patience is what this takes. If you want to *instill* respect, you have to *show* respect. How else to make a partner of something that wants at first only to rebel and run away. These cowboys of our time are not out to subdue their colts, but to come to an understanding with them — a lifelong understanding.

COLLINS   *These horses, they'll be the best friend you ever had.*

If, that is, you have been a friend to them.

On Wade Collins's young horses, you will have noticed, were young riders, mostly. That is because Wade Collins believes that *two-legged* colts need training, too.

# Pilottown

The Mississippi River is one of the great watery roads of the world. But there are no roads at all in the little town from which its bar pilots come. By law, and by long tradition, no ship may go up the Mississippi without a man of Pilottown at its helm. That is because learning the river is more than the work of a lifetime. It's the work of several lifetimes.

Take Mac Lincoln there. His father was a pilot, too. So was *his* father. It takes that long to learn the river.

The ships do not slow down at all as pilots clamber up what always has been called the Jacob's ladder. And then they go calmly to work, guiding seagoing camels through the eye of a needle.

---

LINCOLN  *A thinking man's place.*

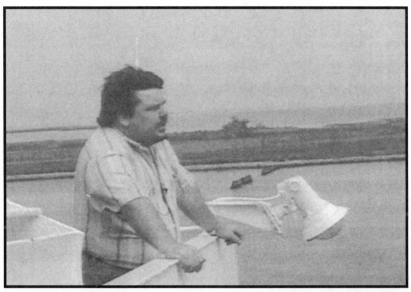

A thinking man's place, of houses on stilts, home to fewer than twenty people, inaccessible except by seaplane or by boat. But then the heart of this country would be inaccessible, too, without the pilots of Pilottown.

An old-time pilot on the Mississippi wrote: "A pilot, in those days, was the only unfettered and entirely independent human being that lived on the Earth." Perhaps in *these* days, too, Mark Twain.

# The Canal

Do you want to know how the West was won *really?* This is how. By a shallow trench cut across the shoulder of New York State from Albany to Buffalo.

Young America felt itself pinched between the eastern mountains and the sea. There was no quick way to move people and goods out into the continent. So in 1817 some American big thinkers had a big thought — the Erie Canal.

Seven years of digging later, on opening day, the Great Lakes and the Atlantic had been joined. The Erie Canal was a wonder of the world.

The city of Syracuse came to look like Venice. Mule-drawn barges came and went at the rate of one every seventeen minutes, all night and all day.

The coming of the railroad ended all this in time, but it was by mule that we were dragged into the future, aboard the flat-bottomed boats they pulled from their towpath alongside the canal. The towpath led to the train; and the train led to the highway, and the highway led to now.

The canalmen were famous roisterers. They say a boy was sent out one day to buy bread and rum for a crew of boatmen. The boy came back with two loaves and one jug, and was beaten — for having bought too much bread.

# Dog Power

KENT HOLMBERG *It's so quiet. Normally all you hear is just breathing.*

Breathing? *Whose* breathing? *Their* breathing. Forget horsepower. Here in Ely, Minnesota, what you need in the wintertime is dog power.

Kent Holmberg took up dogsledding as a pastime when he decided he was too old to ski. Turns out this is a lot harder than skiing. There is as much running as there is riding. But you get to go places no one else can go. And it isn't just Kent and his daughter Ashley who are eager to set out. The dogs are eager, too.

HOLMBERG *They naturally love to run. From little puppies, the minute you leave with the team, the puppies are just dying to go. We'll either let them run alongside or sometimes clip 'em in.*

*Gee* and *haw* are what you say to turn the dogs one way or the other. But mostly you say nothing at all. That is the point — to leave the need for speech as far behind as you can.

Dogsledding is exciting during the day, of course, but try it at night when it's very cold and the snow is very hard. *They* can see well enough, but all *you* can do as you're being whipped through the dark is listen to the sound of great effort up ahead. And great exhilaration.

# Little Fish, Big Buildings

If you think fishing is a country pursuit, look here. This has been going on in Chicago in the right season for as long as anyone can remember. The little fish called smelt come in from the lake, and the urban fishermen turn up, too, to build fires and drop their nets, and to cook their catch right on the spot — when there *is* a catch.

———

MAN *I've caught two smelts in the last four years, and I still come down.*

The fishing has not been good for some seasons now. But they gather anyway, because this is an old tradition, worthy of being passed on to the next generation.

This is what many Chicagoans did when the world was young — took their nets and their children to the water's edge to build fires and try their luck. But for Chicago blazing so beautifully in the background, this might be a picture of an evening at the dawn of time.

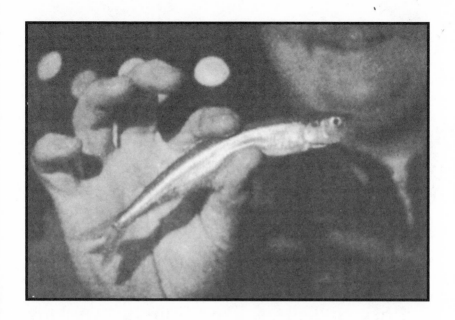

One of the veterans of that far shore of Lake Michigan says he remembers a season not so long ago during which he caught 2,222 smelt — by actual count, he says. And the smelt may come back. But right now the catch is often like Chicago's Michael Jordan shooting a basketball: nothing but net.

# Roll, Cross, and Flip

This is the twisted tale of two towns of Pennsylvania, in which are made — pretzels. And more pretzels. And still more pretzels.

Reading is where the Bachman family does it, and Lititz, Pennsylvania, is where it all began. Tell us, Tom Sturgis, how long has your family been baking pretzels?

STURGIS *If you want to include my father, my grandfather, and my great-grandfather, Julius, it would be since about 1860.*

Julius Sturgis of Lititz was the founding father of the pretzel in this country. And the secret is?

STURGIS *It's just a matter of learning how to do the little flick.*

Now tourists try "the little flick." They fail mostly. And that's the way it goes in central Pennsylvania, pretzel purveyors to America.

Julius Sturgis was first in this country, but first *anywhere* were the monks of old Europe. Not only did they keep learning alive through the Dark Ages and give us brandy. It seems they invented the pretzel, too, as a reminder of prayer. You see, people used to pray with their arms folded across their chests.

*American Notions*

# The Right Tool

Here is Roger Faris of Seattle leading us down to a part of his library. This seems a dim sort of place in which to keep books. But Roger Faris's library is not a library of books. It's a library of tools.

WOMAN  *I want the circle saw.*

FARIS  *Oh, a circular saw. Very good.*

MAN  *I need one of the drills that . . .*

FARIS  *Roto-Hammer.*

The people of the Phinney Neighborhood Association come to this library not to improve their minds, but to improve their homes. Roger Faris takes your name and phone number, and off you go to do battle with tub tiles or with pipes.

FARIS  *This is the kind of wrench that causes plumbing to cooperate.*

And what special cement holds all this together?

FARIS *Yeah, I guess, just trust. So, it's a good thing.*

Did he say *trust?* And you thought trust was the rusted tool of another age. Not here, apparently. Whether you need a lot of help, or just a *bit* . . .

FARIS *Hello, Roger here.*

Librarian of tools, Roger Faris, can help you.

WOMAN *It's the world's best library.*

FARIS *Thank you much.*

"Neither a borrower nor a lender be." That crotchety centuries-old advice is being ignored, cheerfully and successfully, by a whole neighborhood in Seattle, Washington.

# All Downhill from Here

PETIE FISK HOWE *Oh, my word! It was just really scary. But after that, there was nothing like it.*

Petie Fisk Howe is talking about *this*, the very first ski tow in all of this country. In 1934, on Fred Gilbert's hill here in Woodstock, Vermont, some pioneers wrapped a long rope around the wheel of the town tractor and invited people to take hold. Up they went, easy as anything. But for this rope, on this hill, skiing might never have become the pastime of millions.

What goes up must come down, yes. But the going-up was a great effort before that day in 1934, an hour's slog up for every wild slide down of a minute or two. Then a few Vermont tinkerers had a bright idea, and for a while people were more interested in the rope than the slope.

HOWE *This line of people would snake almost down to the barn here, all waiting for this great experience. There was nothing like it.*

There *was* nothing like it. That was the beginning.

Up until 1934 you had to work very hard for the reward of being able to feel the wind in your face on the way down. Now you can feel the wind in your face on the way up, too.

Progress sometimes really is progress.

# A Click Heard
# 'Round the World

Here's one American company that believes
in its product. If you have a Zippo lighter . . .

_____

MICHAEL SCHULER   *It works or we fix it
free.*

There is no fine print. Zippo's lifetime guar-
antee is not for the lifetime of the owner; it's
for the lifetime of the lighter. Whether you
bought it yourself or were left it by your
grandfather or found it in the street where a
truck had run over it, you can send your
Zippo back to Bradford, Pennsylvania, and
they'll fix it free. And if it breaks again,
they'll fix it free again. And so on. Forever.

There are letters of thanks here from
Dwight Eisenhower and from Douglas
MacArthur, and there are *imploring* letters
from Switzerland, from Holland, from all
over.

Our soldiers took these handheld bits of
America to the world once, and the world

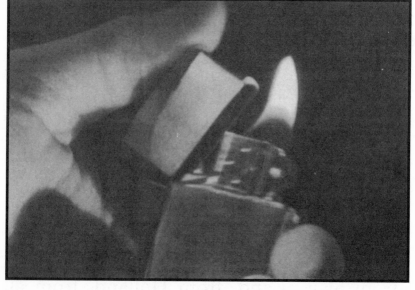

took to them. Zippo president Michael Schuler is understandably proud of this.

SCHULER *The shape of it and the sound of it are recognized throughout the world. When they hear the click of the lid, they say, "Oh, that's a Zippo."*

Zippo doesn't care how your Zippo was damaged. By war. By your power mower. By your cocker spaniel. It doesn't matter.

SCHULER *It works or we fix it free.*

It isn't true, you see, that companies no longer stand behind what they make.
Think of this as the eternal flame.

# Smoke Signals

Do you know what this imposing structure is? It is, basically, a humidor, surrounded by a nightclub: the Living Room of Schaumburg, Illinois. The *draw* here — for women, too — is the draw, if you see what I mean.

You order your cigar from something like a wine list, and the prices are not much different than they might be for wine. Out they come from under lock and key to be brought to you on a silver platter, and then to be custom-cut at one end, and *toasted,* as they say, at the other.

Wait, though — isn't the entire country frowning on smoking just now? It is indeed. But then, the country's frowning produced quite a similar effect, really, once upon a time. This place is a kind of speakeasy of the nineties.

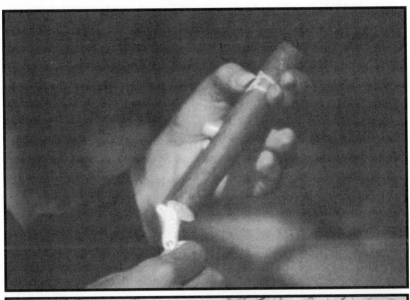

The new popularity of the cigar is a wondrous paradox of this tobacco-despising age of ours. How to explain it? I'm sure I can't. But I do know this much. That old complaint, the one that goes "What this country needs is a good five-cent cigar," will have to be adjusted a lot for inflation.

# And the Cares That Hung Around Me Through the Week

Once upon a time couples danced the night away. Welcome to — once upon a time.

This is the Gulfport Casino of Gulfport, Florida. The best dancers in the world say this is the best dance floor in the world. It's of hard maple and dates from the 1930s. So do *they*, mostly — and the twenties and the teens.

This isn't just a pastime, you know.

---

RAY PLATH *You can dance morning, noon, and night here.*

Ray Plath, once of Boston, was a private investigator. Ever since he retired, he's been keeping an eye on his own fancy footwork.

And lest you think this lovely tradition is sure to fade away when they do — not that they look like fading — notice a certain very young nose pressed up against the glass door of the casino. What do you think he will be doing twenty or forty or sixty years from now? By then this night will be *his* — once upon a time.

I'm no dancer, but I love to watch dancing. The dancer Ted Shawn said, "Dance is the only art where the stuff it's made of is us, ourselves."

# The Music of the Map

"I have fallen in love with American names," wrote the poet Stephen Vincent Benét.

Well, really — how could you not? Not if you've been to Lick Skillet, Texas, and Bug Tussle, and Nip and Tuck, and Cut and Shoot. In California you can travel from Humbug Flat to Lousy Level, with a detour to Gouge Eye.

Could the good people of Sleepy Eye, Minnesota, use some Hot Coffee, Mississippi, to wake them up?

You can go from Matrimony, North Carolina, to Caress, Virginia — or from Caress to Matrimony.

I have passed time in Monkey's Eyebrow, Kentucky, and Bowlegs and Tombstone, Big Chimney and Bull Town. And I liked Dwarf, Kentucky, though it's just a little town.

"I have fallen in love with American names." How could anybody not?

Robert Louis Stevenson was also struck by the wealth upon our maps. He wrote,

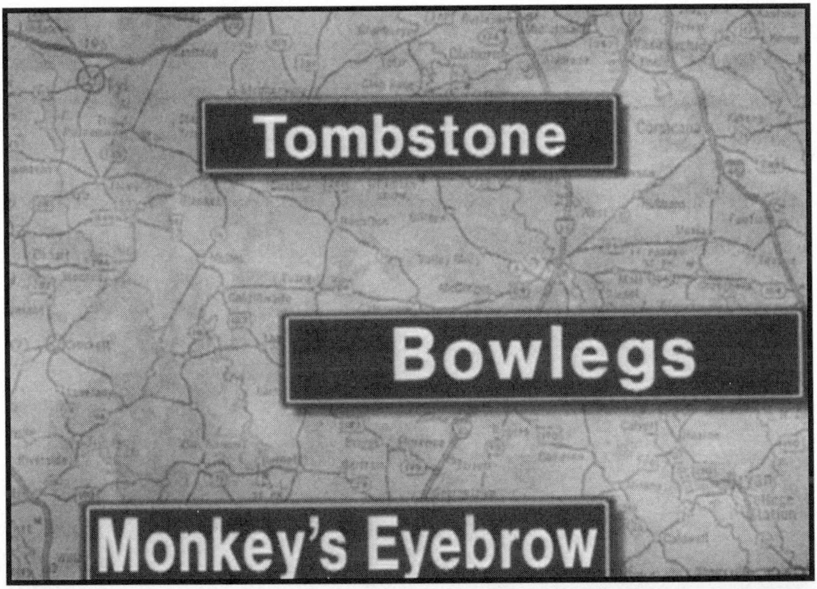
Tombstone
Bowlegs
Monkey's Eyebrow

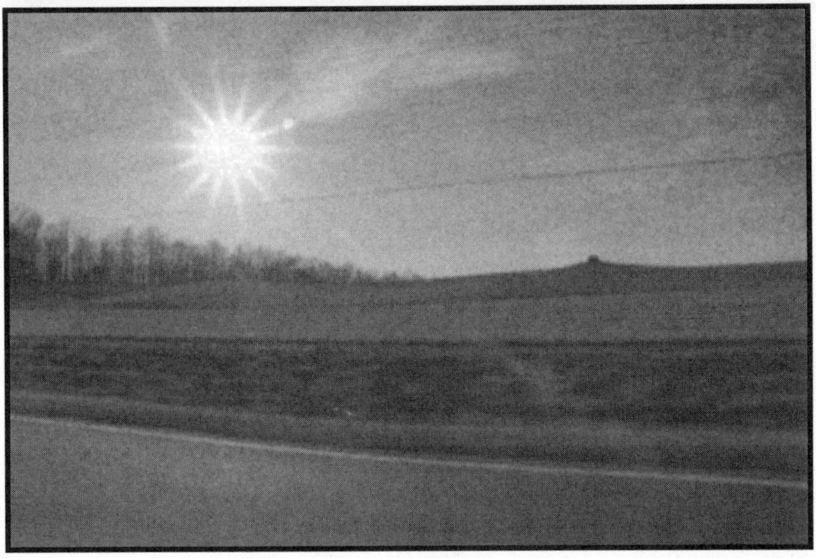

"There is no part of the world where nomenclature is so rich, poetical, humorous, and picturesque, as the United States of America." He called our country a "songful, tuneful land."

# Seeing the Light

This is a story of an old hero of the North Carolina shore — a hero that has been standing at attention on Hatteras Island for a long time now. Park ranger and historian Rob Bolling can tell you about its arrival here.

BOLLING  *This lighthouse was completed in 1870 after about a year and a half of getting bricks down here in the middle of nowhere, getting granite quarried from New England, dragging it across a couple of miles of this island, swatting mosquitoes, having islanders work for twenty-five cents a day — good pay back in 1870 — and getting this thing rising up to be the tallest, at that time, lighthouse in the world.*

Here it rose. And here, pretty soon it will fall — unless it is moved. The sea is approaching, and the sand retreating, in spite of the jetties and the huge sandbags that can only slow the inevitable.

This hero has saved lives, many lives. It has been more reliable than the moon. But the moon can hang in midair. The Hatteras lighthouse cannot.

The Hatteras light isn't *really* needed anymore. But it is historic, and it is beautiful. And you'd think we'd want to stand by something that has stood by us for so long.

# Squinting Scientists

You may do your stargazing at night, but the scientists on this hilltop of New Mexico do theirs during the day.

---

STEVEN KYLE  *I see the sun as a big unstable ball of gas up in the sky.*

Well, yes, that's what a star is — which is why Steven Kyle and his colleagues at the National Solar Observatory keep all their many telescopic eyes trained upon it from sunrise to sunset every day of the year. It's this way: the eye of heaven *winks* sometimes. Come then solar flares, great wild eruptions of energy that foul things up here on earth. Satellite communications go haywire. Electrical power is interrupted. The job in Sunspot, New Mexico, is to understand sunspots.

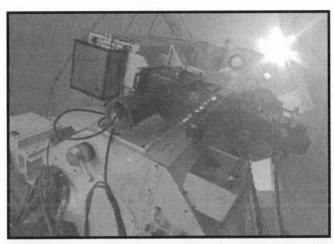

KYLE *This is an image of the sun, here is the rim of the sun, so if there were a sun flare going on here at the edge, you would probably see something sticking out here.*

They do not have it figured out just yet. But never you mind. In Sunspot, New Mexico, every day in every way, things are looking up.

Nothing much was happening away up there on our star the day we visited the National Solar Observatory. There were no million-mile outbursts of temper out into space. That day, on the sun, it was just — sunny.

# Winter's Wild Rides

Have you noticed how many ways there are these days to go down a hill? The *old* way involved wood and metal.

As for the new ways, there are sleds of plastic, and saucers, and doughnuts. You can go down on your back, or on your belly. Feet first, or head first. You can lose your hat, or your dignity. You can go down the hill by yourself, or in groups of two, or three, or four.

Sleds can be arranged fore-and-aft. Or raft-style, side-by-side. Piggyback is a possibility, too. However you slide down, though, you still have to get back up again. And that can be tricky.

If anything like this were to happen to us by accident, we would hate it, of course. But, if we *choose* to go hurtling down a hill, that makes it fun, great fun, and accounts for that uniquely broad "sledder's smile," which is caused by a mixture of cold wind in the face, and just a little hint of fear.

What would winter be without a wild ride down a steep hill?

# About Time

Look here. Time does not fly. It *chirps*. And sails. And passes in review to be blessed. This is the Time Museum of Rockford, Illinois, dedicated not so much to time as it is to time machines, and to the stunning ingenuity of their makers.

Time is silent, in fact — but not here. Time is invisible, in fact — but not here.

And time cannot really be divided, in fact. But human beings have divided it, with wheels and weights and teeth and cogs, into very fine slivers indeed. Just look at this

intricate clockwork, centuries of it, all for weighing what is weightless, and for measuring the immeasurable. Think how much time we've spent giving form to formless time.

If you are looking for American Moments, then the ticking town of Rockford, Illinois, is the place for you.

# On Paper Wings

If you want some measure of how much affection there is in this country, this is where you come around Valentine's Day, to watch the printing presses of the Hallmark Company in Kansas City.

Cupid's wings flutter very fast in February. He has millions of cards to deliver. Out of the presses all day and all night come pledges of love — polite, platonic, passionate, sassy, sentimental, clever, coy. They will be signed, many of them. But then some will say only "Guess Who," or "Secret Admirer."

There are antique cards on display here, too — the intricate and lacy missives of another time. But they are not bound anywhere. All of the others are. Really, this is one of the great annual migrations — of heartfelt sentiment, from Kansas City to every other city and small town of America.

For many years there was *another* tradition on Valentine's Day, of cards with rhymed insults. These grew so rude that they were ultimately banned in many places

by about 1850. "Vinegar Valentines," they were called.

So, if ever the sweetness of February in our day seems a bit much to you, think what *might* be in your mailbox.

# The Road Less Traveled

If ever you grow weary of the modern world, take a turn toward Vermont, where the pavement ends. Vermonters are devoted to their thousands of miles of unpaved roads — and Vermonter Howard Jillson Coffin can tell you why.

COFFIN *First they love the rutted path, I think, because it's the way things used to be, and not the way things are becoming.*

In Vermont, they call it "preventing the future." An unpaved road keeps you from driving too fast, or forgetting too fast.

COFFIN *Some of the most wonderful people that ever inhabited the earth lived in these hills and hollows. We don't have enough of those people today. We remember those things when we're on a back road.*

Robert Frost, the poet of New England, wrote about the charms of the road less traveled. Surely, that was an unpaved road — maybe this one.

We are in a great rush now, of course. But we used to meander, just as the dirt roads of Vermont still do.

On the unbending interstate, you can see the future ahead of you, many, many miles ahead. On a dirt road, however, you can see something better than that. You can see the past.

# Acknowledgments

Charles Kuralt would have been the first to explain at the outset that television is not made by individuals. Think of something like an old-fashioned traveling circus. Of the traveling circus represented here, Charles was the guiding spirit and the ringmaster. I was, at most, company pamphleteer. And then Claire Chiappetta was everything else — roustabout, wrangler, rope and wagon master, lion and logistics tamer, and seer to all other needful matters large and small.

But then even Claire's Herculean efforts would have been for naught without the contributions of all those who trooped about the country, putting their lenses and their microphones in exactly the right place every time — however hard the right place may have been to get to, or to stay in — and who often enough conducted the conversations quoted in this book. I salute and thank them all (in alphabetical order): Greg Bader, Randall Blakey, Isadore Bleckman, Skip Brand, Ray Bribiesca, Skip Brown, Dan Collison, Pat Craft, Todd Doane, Al Durruthy, John Duvall, Aaron Frutman, Dean Gaskill, Danny Gianneschi, Carl Gilman, Mark Honer, Henry Kokojan, Joe La-Monaco, Sid Lubitsch, Joanne Mc-

Donough, Tom Magill, John Maher, Harvey Marshall, Cleve Massey, Tony Pagano, Eric Prentnieks, Lynn Rabren, Derek Reich, Dan Sack, Bob Thibault, and Rus Thompson. And I salute those wonderful editors Jeff Hutton and Jason Yowell, who took the pictures and the sound the little company above provided and turned those pictures and that sound into beautifully polished gems.

To Ninth Wave Productions, and most especially to Jim Kirk and Neal Spelce thereat, thank you for putting your shoulders against the stones that Charles and I must have seemed at first, to get all this moving and to keep all this moving.

And to Greg Bellon, friend and agent of Charles Kuralt, and now friend and agent of mine, many thanks for many kinds of help.

At Simon & Schuster, I bow low before Annik La Farge, editor extraordinaire, and Amy Hill, designer extraordinaire, whose alchemy has turned the airborne ephemera of television into a book that is uncommonly lovely to look down into.

Finally, for her extraordinary graciousness at a time when, in mourning, she had every right to turn away from any and all requests, I offer profound thanks to Charles's wife, Suzanne Kuralt, for letting this book happen.

11 sw
23x